T0289876

AI-Powered
Bitcoin Trading

AI-Powered Bitcoin Trading

Developing an Investment Strategy with Artificial Intelligence

Eoghan Leahy

WILEY

For general information on our other products and services or for technical support, please contact our Customer Care Department within the United States at (800) 762-2974, outside the United States at (317) 572-3993 or fax (317) 572-4002.

Wiley also publishes its books in a variety of electronic formats. Some content that appears in print may not be available in electronic formats. For more information about Wiley products, visit our web site at www.wiley.com.

Library of Congress Cataloging-in-Publication Data is Available:

ISBN 9781119661177 (Hardback)
ISBN 9781119661221 (ePDF)
ISBN 9781119661160 (ePub)

Cover Design: Wiley
Cover Image: © grafius/Adobe Stock

SKY10072525_041524

Contents

Contents

Chapter 1

The Block of Genesis

"The Times 03/Jan/2009 Chancellor on brink of second bailout for banks."

—Satoshi Nakamoto

The birth of Bitcoin, like many religious movements, is a story for the ages. Bitcoin was founded by one mythical individual whose impact may last centuries. While there have been many false idols and pretenders to the crown, Bitcoin has remained the core of the cryptocurrency movement.

The exact birth date of Bitcoin can be disputed. The initial whitepaper was published on an online cryptographic forum on Halloween 2008. However, the timestamp of the first block is technically at 18:15:15 UTC on January 3, 2009, yet the Bitcoin network did not go live until January 8.

Satoshi Nakamoto is a pseudonym adopted by Bitcoin's creator, whose real identity has never been publicly revealed. There is something magical about a new disruptive financial ecosystem being launched by a single unknown operator who has never claimed the wealth they created.

Bitcoin: A Peer-to-Peer Electronic Cash System

Satoshi Nakamoto
satoshin@gmx.com
www.bitcoin.org

Abstract. A purely peer-to-peer version of electronic cash would allow online payments to be sent directly from one party to another without going through a financial institution. Digital signatures provide part of the solution, but the main benefits are lost if a trusted third party is still required to prevent double-spending. We propose a solution to the double-spending problem using a peer-to-peer network. The network timestamps transactions by hashing them into an ongoing chain of hash-based proof-of-work, forming a record that cannot be changed without redoing the proof-of-work. The longest chain not only serves as proof of the sequence of events witnessed, but proof that it came from the largest pool of CPU power. As long as a majority of CPU power is controlled by nodes that are not cooperating to attack the network, they'll generate the longest chain and outpace attackers. The network itself requires minimal structure. Messages are broadcast on a best effort basis, and nodes can leave and rejoin the network at will, accepting the longest proof-of-work chain as proof of what happened while they were gone.

Figure 1.1   The original Bitcoin whitepaper.

Many books have been written trying to decipher the real identity of Satoshi. Exhaustive analysis of the original emails between Satoshi and early adopters from the cryptocurrency community reveals some critical information.

Studying the email time zones, the writing styles, and comments made by counterparties offers clues. Early messages question whether Satoshi is even Japanese, as the name would suggest. Some have claimed to be Satoshi, and some still do, but to date, no irrefutable proof has been tabled.

While the "who" of Bitcoin is uncertain, the why is much more obvious. Encoded by Satoshi in the first-ever Bitcoin transaction was the following message:

The Times 03/Jan/2009 Chancellor on brink of second bailout for banks.

The above statement is a reference to the bailout of the global banking industry during the financial crisis of 2008/2009. The decision by governments to socialize the losses of private institutions marked the death of the fiat currency system. The profits of banks are private; however, the government covered their losses. In doing so, it passed the burden on to the public citizens through taxes and inflation caused by reckless money printing.

```
00000000   01 00 00 00 00 00 00 00   00 00 00 00 00 00 00 00   ................
00000010   00 00 00 00 00 00 00 00   00 00 00 00 00 00 00 00   ................
00000020   00 00 00 00 3B A3 ED FD   7A 7B 12 B2 7A C7 2C 3E   ....;£íýz{.²zÇ,>
00000030   67 76 8F 61 7F C8 1B C3   88 8A 51 32 3A 9F B8 AA   gv.a.È.Ã^šQ2:Ÿ.ª
00000040   4B 1E 5E 4A 29 AB 5F 49   FF FF 00 1D 1D AC 2B 7C   K.^J)«_Iÿÿ...¬+|
00000050   01 01 00 00 00 01 00 00   00 00 00 00 00 00 00 00   ................
00000060   00 00 00 00 00 00 00 00   00 00 00 00 00 00 00 00   ................
00000070   00 00 00 00 00 00 FF FF   FF FF 4D 04 FF FF 00 1D   ......ÿÿÿÿM.ÿÿ..
00000080   01 04 45 54 68 65 20 54   69 6D 65 73 20 30 33 2F   ..EThe Times 03/
00000090   4A 61 6E 2F 32 30 30 39   20 43 68 61 6E 63 65 6C   Jan/2009 Chancel
000000A0   6C 6F 72 20 6F 6E 20 62   72 69 6E 6B 20 6F 66 20   lor on brink of
000000B0   73 65 63 6F 6E 64 20 62   61 69 6C 6F 75 74 20 66   second bailout f
000000C0   6F 72 20 62 61 6E 6B 73   FF FF FF FF 01 00 F2 05   or banksÿÿÿÿ..ò.
000000D0   2A 01 00 00 00 43 41 04   67 8A FD B0 FE 55 48 27   *....CA.gŠý°þUH'
000000E0   19 67 F1 A6 71 30 B7 10   5C D6 A8 28 E0 39 09 A6   .gñ¦q0·.\Ö¨(à9.¦
000000F0   79 62 E0 EA 1F 61 DE B6   49 F6 BC 3F 4C EF 38 C4   ybàê.aÞ¶Iö¼?Lï8Ä
00000100   F3 55 04 E5 1E C1 12 DE   5C 38 4D F7 BA 0B 8D 57   óU.å.Á.Þ\8M÷º..W
00000110   8A 4C 70 2B 6B F1 1D 5F   AC 00 00 00 00            ŠLp+kñ._¬....
```

Figure 1.2   The genesis block's hexadecimal code.

Bitcoin supply is finite. This means that no person or entity can create more to benefit themselves at the expense of all that rely on the currency as a store of value. This is a key feature of Bitcoin relative to most other cryptocurrency projects.

This means that no government can print more Bitcoin to bail out corporations or fund wars. Essentially, the fiat money system allows politicians to write checks that the rest of the population needs to pay for, a problem that has now become so severe that for the debt to be repaid in full, it may be that future generations will have to pay the price for the financial recklessness of a few.

The chart of the total assets of the US Federal Reserve shows a parabolic rise, growing ten times from an initial base of under $1 trillion (USD) since 2013. The growth in the US national debt when compared to national GDP is reaching dangerous levels.

Paul Tudor Jones laid out the investment case for investors in the May 2020 BVI Macro Outlook. He discussed the inflationary pressures caused by the FED's money-printing policies, stating that:

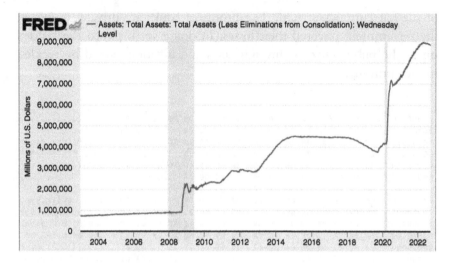

Figure 1.3   FRED: total assets.
Source: FRED / https://fred.stlouisfed.org/series/WALCL / Public Domain.

The current economic environment presents a compelling opportunity to explore how Bitcoin can be part of a resilient portfolio. As demand for stores of value grows during this regime of monetary inflation, Bitcoin may be well-positioned given that it is a scarce digital asset. (Paul Tudor Jones, 2020)

The current levels of debt have passed the event horizon. There is no realistic way for this debt to be repaid. A new financial reset is likely, and Bitcoin may well be at the core of the eventual solution.

Bitcoin was not just created to control the destruction of value by central bank money printing. It attacks the core of the financial system. Money is created as debt, and debt incurs interest. So as soon as money is created and interest is owed, there is no longer enough money in the system to settle all debts. Furthermore, with charges placed on financial transactions, this pool of money shrinks further.

In the past, financial security was an important issue. Individuals needed a place to keep their money safe from theft, while international transactions were complicated and took considerable time.

Advances such as the Internet, artificial intelligence, faster computer processing speeds, cryptography, cybersecurity, and international

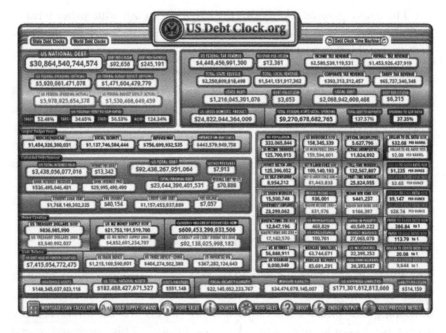

Figure 1.4 US Debt Clock.
Source: https://www.usdebtclock.org/.

commerce are now more effective and efficient at keeping money safe and transacting quickly and securely. Satoshi clearly highlights that the core purpose of Bitcoin is to remove the financial sector involvement from the money system using digital currencies built on blockchain technology that use mathematics for security rather than physical vaults.

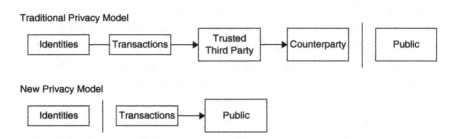

Figure 1.5 Bitcoin was designed to remove financial institutions from transactions.

The above graphic taken from the original Bitcoin whitepaper written by Satoshi unceremoniously cuts "trusted third parties" and "counterparties" out of the financial transaction process.

"What is needed is an electronic payment system based on cryptographic proof instead of trust, allowing any two willing parties to transact directly with each other without the need for a trusted third party" (Satoshi, Bitcoin whitepaper).

It is clear to see why the traditional financial sector views Bitcoin and cryptocurrency as an existential threat to the current global payments system—because it is!

An Immutable Ledger

The blockchain ledger is like a Bible that can't be rewritten. In the past decade, the language of some versions of the Bible has changed from describing the interactions of Jesus with "lepers" to the more socially acceptable "people with rare skin conditions." This increased social awareness, while likely in line with the sentiment of the original authors, is not the exact word-for-word writings of the original author.

What if there was a way to secure data so that it can never be changed in the future? That is exactly how an immutable ledger works. This provides the security authentication layer that underlies blockchain technology.

Bitcoin Mining

The first Bitcoin block was mined in January 2009. Like any sector, cryptocurrency has a high level of obfuscation (a word that often does what it means), as it is heavy with jargon taken from several different disciplines such as trading, finance, technology, gaming, and coding, to name a few. The sector has also created its own new set of terms to increase the "FUD" (fear, uncertainty, and doubt) that deters traders from "HODLing" (holding on for dear life).

The key is to stay humble and not let a lack of knowledge discourage your investment in the cryptocurrency space. Instead, dedicate yourself to learning. In fact, it is the early adopters who take the most risk early in projects that get rewarded the most. The future of cryptocurrency definitely favors the brave.

The earliest of those adopters that are constantly rewarded are the miners. So what is Bitcoin mining, and how does it work?

Bitcoin supply is fixed at 21 million Bitcoin—no more can ever be created. It is this finite supply that directly addresses the central bank currency debasement issue. Each Bitcoin is divisible by eight places after the decimal point (0.00000001 BTC), while the smallest unit is called a Satoshi, or sat for brevity.

There are several problems to be solved to launch and maintain a digital currency such as Bitcoin. How do you mint the currency over time in a controlled way that will not lead to liquidity issues that affect price stability? How do you incentivize others to help you maintain the immutable ledger and process transactions on the blockchain 24/7/365? How do you keep the network secure from hackers and bad operators?

The problems above are addressed by the intricate details involved in the mining process. Bitcoin uses a mining mechanism called proof of work, which requires miners to apply computer processing power to try and solve complex mathematical problems to earn newly minted Bitcoin. While mining to earn Bitcoin, they simultaneously settle Bitcoin transactions, communicate periodically with other miners to "validate" the transactions are correct, and add them to the immutable ledger of transactions on the Bitcoin blockchain.

Imagine a college lecturer in an auditorium with 100 students. Not the most tech-savvy operator, they write lecture notes by hand, copying verbatim what is written by the professor on a chalkboard. Occasionally, the lecturer makes spelling errors, as do some of the students. One day the lecturer's notebook gets stolen! The sole centralized storage of all vital information is lost forever—what a disaster!

The students suggest that the lecturer could reconstruct the book by using the notes the students had taken. The lecturer was able to work through the information again with the students able to validate if there were any errors. Any time there was a query, they could take a majority vote to resolve issues. In this way by distributing the document, its information was saved despite the corruption of the centralized database—the lecturer's notebook. Similarly, errors were removed by adding a voting consensus mechanism to resolve potential errors, gaps, and disputes.

What would happen if over 51% of the students decided to play a prank on the lecturer and change some of the words in the teachings? There may be a dispute, but the bad operators would have a majority and be able to corrupt the ledger.

A short answer to this problem is that you want to ensure that each individual node is secure from corruption, and the more participants you have, the more secure the network. This is a key concept in cryptocurrency and blockchain technology known as "decentralization."

The Blockchain Trilemma

The trade-off between decentralization, security, and scalability is referred to as the "blockchain trilemma," a term made popular by Vitalik Buterin (Ethereum cofounder). It refers to the trade-offs between the objectives of a blockchain ecosystem with regard to transaction speed, measured in transactions per second (TPS).

"While Visa can process up to 24,000 transactions per second (TPS), Bitcoin can only process seven TPS, and Ethereum can handle 20 TPS. Cryptocurrencies must catch up with Visa's capability to achieve mass adoption" (crypto.com).

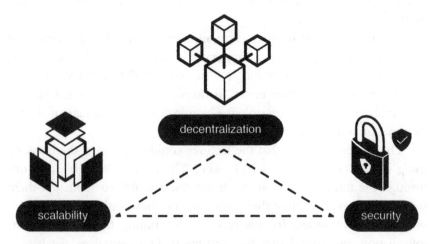

Figure 1.6   Scalability, decentralization, and security.
Source: Adapted from https://www.ledger.com/academy/what-is-the-blockchain-trilemma.

Why is Bitcoin considered the best cryptocurrency if it is so slow for processing transactions? Is it not supposed to be a transactions network?

The reason Bitcoin is so comparably slow is that it sacrifices speed to increase security. This is the reason Bitcoin is referred to as a "layer 0" blockchain. It provides the protocols, hardware, miners, etc., that secure the ecosystem.

The trilemma suggests that to improve one of the three objectives, sacrifices must be made that negatively affect the other priorities. For example, changes that may increase the transaction speed may compromise security.

Security

The entire security of Bitcoin relies on mathematics, cryptography, and computer code. They literally put the "crypto" in "cryptocurrency." It is alarming how few people that own crypto or work in the cryptocurrency space understand the underlying cryptography that secures their investment.

Let us undertake a quick overview of the cryptography and security protocols that secure the Bitcoin network and protect the wallets and coins of investors. Having an understanding of, and confidence in, the encryption and authentication processes drive the trust and adoption of investors in cryptocurrencies and digital assets.

In the next chapter, we will discuss blockchain technology and hacking in more detail. We now understand that much of the security from the encryption used in blockchain and Bitcoin comes from creating complex problems that current computers are not fast enough to solve. The protection comes from the use of secret cryptographic keycodes that are too large and complex to decipher in a short enough period of time for bad operators to break the encryption.

Each individual data package and wallet has a digital signature for communicating, and these rely on cryptographic hash keys. Should a package be corrupted, the onus is on the rest of the network validators to recognize this and destroy the block.

To protect the entire network from being overtaken by a 51% attack (more on this later), the network draws strength from the decentralization of its participants. More participants increase the total hash rate of the network, making it more secure from an attack that would take over the whole network, allowing the bad operators full control of the consensus mechanism, allowing them to publish false blocks of transactions, etc.

Decentralization and scalability are goals that if achieved, will drive the capabilities of the blockchain to attract more participants, in a positive feedback loop. Security on the other hand is paramount; without it, the whole system fails. The inability to protect the data package encryption from attack as well as the network as a whole may result in bad operators falsifying transactions, stealing funds, or taking over the network entirely.

Scalability

Scalability is all about enhancing the speed of the blockchain so that it can offer better capabilities to its users. However, this may often come at the expense of decentralization and security.

Centralized payment systems operate at impressive numbers of transactions per second, which is easier to accomplish with a closed, private network. A closed network is not as exposed to bad operators and hackers as an open-source code, public blockchain is. The ability of a blockchain to scale and decentralize successfully improves security; the challenge is finding the right balance between these three objectives to attract participants without compromising security.

Notice how Bitcoin cannot process more than seven transactions per second, which is a long way behind the 24,000 TPS recorded by Visa. The speed of bitcoin and other blockchains depends on the way the networks operate. Bitcoin, as previously explained, is more concerned with security than transaction volumes.

As a blockchain attracts more participants, it becomes more decentralized, which is good. However, if there are too many participants, then there will be a transaction bottleneck, which may result in errors, high transaction costs, or slow service. Restricting the number of participants would ease the burden on the network but reduce decentralization, which affects security and scalability.

There is no magic solution to resolve this issue, although some blockchains suggest they have made strong advances. The industry is still too new and untested to verify their claims. Some known methods that can

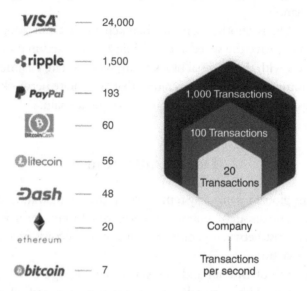

Figure 1.7 Cryptocurrency transaction speeds compared to Visa & Paypal.
Source: Adapted from https://crypto.com/university/blockchain-scalability#:~:text=
The%20Transaction%20Speed%20of%20Cryptocurrencies&text=While%20Visa%20
can%20process%20up,capability%20to%20achieve%20mass%20adoption.

help increase TPS performance include sharding, adopting layer 2 solutions, using sidechains, and altering the consensus mechanism.

Sharding involves splitting the data into smaller partitioned blockchains,
called "shards." Each shard can process transactions independently with
interactions between shards controlled by a main "beacon" blockchain.
This layer of network activity helps improve performance.

As discussed, the reason Bitcoin's TPS is so slow is to ensure security
through what is referred to as a proof-of-work consensus mechanism. Essentially this refers to the way that new blocks of information are validated by
participants. Changes to the consensus mechanism can have a large impact
on the performance of the blockchain. An example of the impact of such a
change was highlighted by the migration of the Ethereum blockchain from
proof of work to proof of stake (more on this in the next chapter).

Changing the consensus mechanism or implementing sharding
involves changes to the fundamental design of the network. Another
option is to build solutions on top of the existing infrastructure that

interacts with the original layer 1 blockchain. Examples include sidechains and state channels.

A sidechain is another separate blockchain that can adopt different methods to improve the speed and scalability of transaction processing and then interacts with the original blockchain, while a state channel processes transactions using smart contracts rather than a separate network to process transactions and report results back to the original chain.

Decentralization

The current global financial system relies on the centralization of data and trade settlement through central counterparties. Essentially it is the banks that enforce trust between people by maintaining records of accounts and clearing transactions.

At the core of Bitcoin and blockchain technology is the concept of decentralization. The network code is open source and all are free to participate. No individual entity is in charge; rather, control is distributed across the network, with all participants having access to the same information.

A benefit of proof of work (PoW) is it promotes increased decentralization, which secures the network. Having more independent blockchain validators dispersed across geographic regions, countries, legal jurisdictions, etc. decreases the dependence of the network on any given person, country, or entity. This provides increased security and makes the likelihood of interference or interruption by third parties or governments less likely.

By dividing the data across multiple participating nodes, the data is more secure from hacking and corruption than if it is stored centrally in a single location. By distributing information across many computers, geographies, and entities, it increases the security of the network, not unlike the concept of diversification in portfolio management theory.

With PoW blockchains, if a single entity were to control over 51% of the computing power, then it would be theoretically possible to try and take over the network and corrupt the ledger. This was a real risk in 2019 when China dominated over 70% of the Bitcoin mining hash power.

China would eventually ban Bitcoin mining, causing the share of mining capacity attributed to China to drop to about 20% of the total. This actually led to a more even distribution of mining power by country (see chart below), which has increased the decentralization of the Bitcoin network, enhancing security and reducing the likelihood of attacks from hackers.

Figure 1.8   Reachable Bitcoin nodes.
Source: Adapted from https://bitnodes.io/#google_vignette.

Top 10 countries with their respective number of reachable nodes are as follow.

RANK	COUNTRY	NODES
1	n/a	4581 (39.20%)
2	United States	1930 (16.52%)
3	Germany	1421 (12.16%)
4	France	461 (3.95%)
5	Netherlands	383 (3.28%)
6	Canada	312 (2.67%)
7	Finland	242 (2.07%)
8	United Kingdom	232 (1.99%)
9	Russian Federation	181 (1.55%)
10	Singapore	152 (1.30%)

Figure 1.9   Top 10 countries with reachable Bitcoin nodes.
Source: Adapted from https://bitnodes.io/#google_vignette.

From Web 2.0 to Web 3.0

The Internet today can be referred to as Web 2.0, a network of websites and applications that are centrally controlled. For example, a content creator can broadcast their own video on YouTube, but to do so they give away their intellectual property and pay a large amount of the revenue they generate to the hosting site.

With decentralization, it will be possible for individuals to own and control their own content and transact peer-to-peer using crypto wallets and direct transactions. This eliminates the need for centrally controlled entities such as banks or Google to be involved in the process. This peer-to-peer network that operates on decentralized platforms is what is referred to as Web 3.0.

The ability of developers to find innovative solutions to solve the blockchain trilemma is key to driving adoption that will facilitate the success of blockchain technology to migrate from Web 2.0 to Web 3.0. Bitcoin and blockchain technology are still in their infancy and have many challenges ahead to reach their potential. As more people adopt cryptocurrencies and blockchain technology, the power of the network grows.

The blockchain trilemma gives a holistic overview of the challenges faced when implementing blockchain technology. Let us dive deeper into the working of Bitcoin and blockchains in the next section to better understand how Bitcoin works and the technology on which the cryptocurrency is built.

Chapter 2

How Bitcoin Works

"Bitcoin is the most important invention in the history of the world since the Internet."

—*Roger Ver*

The following explanation of the workings of Bitcoin is designed for simplicity—we will not dwell on details. The focus of this book is the trading of Bitcoin prices, not the analysis of how it functions.

Extensive books have been written on each section topic to which we will allocate just a few paragraphs. The goal is to move quickly from A to Z, giving a holistic overview of how Bitcoin works so that readers are comfortable investing in the sector.

The fact that we will not dwell on these topics in this book does not excuse investors from studying these topics in more depth. Despite people constantly advising others to "just buy some Bitcoin, put it away, and forget about it," that strategy has not proven to be the most effective since 2017. Many trends have come and gone in the cryptocurrency space just as cryptocurrency has its macro considerations and cyclical forces.

We will run through the key concepts to provide a base level of understanding of the underlying fundamentals and workings of Bitcoin. We want to cover our bases and then move quickly onto the core focus of the book, which is price analysis and the development of trading and investment strategies.

Blockchain Technology

Much fanfare has been made of the potential applications of blockchain technology since the inception of Bitcoin and the explosion of awareness (and investment) around its potential future applications. Essentially a blockchain is a way of decentralizing the data storage, analysis, and distribution process. Instead of a centralized storage database that secures and processes information, these tasks are divided among participating computers referred to as "nodes." This transition from centralization to decentralization has both strengths and weaknesses, and in many instances, there are compromises to be made, as outlined in the blockchain trilemma.

We have given a brief introduction in Chapter 1 to some of the technology and concepts that underlie Bitcoin. Now is the time to run through some of these concepts in more detail. Once you understand the working concepts on which Bitcoin has been developed, you will have more confidence in investing in the sector.

There are different ways for blockchains to operate in relation to how crypto rewards are distributed to the validators who process the transactions. These operational considerations also determine how well the blockchain functions in terms of security, speed, decentralization, and utility.

A key benefit of distributing information across several participating computers is security. Having multiple backups of information prevents loss but also secures against corruption. If you had 100 participating nodes all validating the same transactions every ten minutes and the security of a node is breached and the information about the transactions is corrupted, it will not be accepted when all the nodes share and cross-validate information.

Nodes communicate and agree on a consensus for the information to be added to the blockchain based on a majority (usually ≥ 51%). If an attacker was able to corrupt over 51% of nodes and change the information before the nodes cross-validate information, it would be possible to take control of the blockchain and corrupt the information about transactions. This is referred to as a "51% attack" and highlights how having more validators that increase decentralization fortifies the security of the network.

Elliptic Curve Cryptography

Bitcoin uses an encryption method referred to as elliptic curve digital signature algorithm (ECDSA). It uses a randomly generated private key (32 bytes), usually a wallet address. That private key corresponds to a public key that must be accompanied by a signature (hash). Then the cryptographic handshake is complete, and access may be granted. The mathematics behind the key generation using elliptic curves is a little complicated but is worth further investigation if you are a fan of mathematics.

Examples of Elliptic Curves

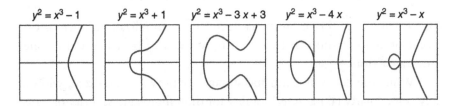

$$y^2 = x^3 - 1 \qquad y^2 = x^3 + 1 \qquad y^2 = x^3 - 3x + 3 \qquad y^2 = x^3 - 4x \qquad y^2 = x^3 - x$$

Figure 2.1   Elliptic curves.
Source: https://hackernoon.com/what-is-the-math-behind-elliptic-curve-cryptography-f61b25253da3.

Satoshi selected an elliptic curve called secp256k1. The secp256k1 curve is pictured in Figure 2.2 and is written in the form: $y^2 = x^3 + 7$.

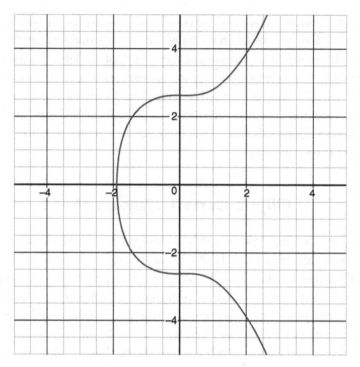

Figure 2.2   Elliptic curve secp256k1.

Cryptocurrency Storage

Blockchains may thrive on the concept of decentralization. There is one point of centralization that leads to most security breaches and erroneous transactions—*you!*

While the data validation and storage are now decentralized, without any central party taking responsibility for the validity and security of transactions, the responsibility is passed on to the owner. If you accidentally send your crypto to an incorrect wallet by accident, there is presently no legal recourse for getting it back.

This individual responsibility for securing your wallet should not be taken lightly. It highlights the need for everyone to educate themselves to safely manage their finances and data.

Hot vs. Cold Storage Wallets

If you store your Bitcoin or other coins with an online broker such as Binance or Kraken, then you do not actually own the Bitcoin, meaning you do not have the private keys, although you do have a legal claim over your assets, especially if you have transferred money from a bank, completed KYC (know your client), and are dealing with a reputable exchange. Storing your crypto in this way is referred to as using a "hot" wallet, so-called as your crypto is being stored online and in theory, is at risk from online hackers.

The other alternative is to store your private keys for your crypto offline on a storage device or to keep them locally on a phone or computer, for example. All methods come with different risks and exposures.

Not to be underestimated is the risk that you play in offline storage. The history of Bitcoin is littered with stories of flash drives with Bitcoin private keys being thrown in landfills or lost forever when a spouse dies but doesn't share the passwords necessary to access them. Ideally, storing offline is theoretically the safer, more libertarian option. Just have a clear plan of how you will store the information and passwords.

What is your backup plan in the event something happens to you? All eventualities should be carefully considered. If you are not confident you can manage offline storage, there are plenty of reputable exchanges with good security protocols that keep the majority of client crypto offline in secure cold wallets with security procedures individuals could never afford to carry out.

Sybil Attacks

Unceremoniously named after an actress who was diagnosed with multiple personality disorder, Sybil attacks refer to an attempt to take control of a network. The hacker creates multiple entities to coordinate a group attack against a system.

An example is the ability of chatbots to generate multiple accounts and dominate a chatroom, effectively drowning out the real participants. This creates what is known as a DDoS (distributed denial of service) attack, where a service is overwhelmed by activity that disrupts normal service for users, by using multiple "Sybil identities."

The aforementioned 51% attack, where a network is taken over by hackers and corrupted or destroyed, is another example of a Sybil attack. Once the network has been compromised, the hackers could change transactions and double-spend cryptocurrency.

To deter such attacks a blockchain must implement processes that discourage bad operators. These procedures are referred to as a "Sybil resistance mechanism," which requires validators of the blockchain to have skin in the game, meaning that there is a cost for participating in the network, which deters large-scale attacks. For example, the amount of computing power that would be needed to carry out a 51% attack on the Bitcoin blockchain is so expensive that it would prove prohibitive.

The goals of the Sybil resistance mechanism are:

1. Create a consensus among participating nodes through a process such as mining (or staking);
2. Create a cost of participation that dissuades scale attacks;
3. Punish bad actors; and
4. Reward honest participants for reaching a consensus and adding a block to the chain.

Consensus Method Mechanism

The term "consensus mechanism" refers to rules that define how agreement takes place between nodes in a blockchain with regard to how blocks communicate and validate the transactions to be added to the blockchain.

Bitcoin uses a "chain selection rule" known as the Nakamoto-style consensus. This rule asserts that whichever blockchain is the longest true state of the immutable transaction ledger will be accepted by the nodes and committed to the chain. There are many other consensus methods employed by other blockchains, but that is outside the scope of this book. What is important to understand is that combining a Sybil resistance

Sybil Resistance Mechanism Overview

Sybil Resistance Mechanism	Competition	Method	Penalty for Misbehavior	Market Dominance
Proof-of-Work (PoW)	Computational work	Solve mathematical puzzles using computational hardware	Proposing an invalid block results in wasted time, energy, and money	58%
Proof-of-Stake (PoS)	Financial stake	Lock up funds in a smart contract	The protocol can destroy a validator's stake or bar from participating in consensus if they fail to step up when called upon or sign invalid brocks	12%
Other*	-	-	-	30%
Non-PoW/PoS Sybil resistance mechanism examples, including but not limited to:				
Proof-of-Authority (PoA)	Reputation	Validators undergo authentication to participate	The protocol can exclude nodes that cheat or go offline from consensus and the consortium of approved validators can impose other penalties	
Proof-of-Space (PoSp)	Disk space	Solve mathematical puzzles by dedicating disk space	The protocol can destroy a validator's stake or bar them from participating in consensus if they fail to step up when called upon or sign invalid blocks	
Proof-of-elapsed Time (PoET)	Fair lottery	Each node must wait for a randomly chosen period; the first to complete the designated waiting time wins the new block	Since PoET is designed for permissioned blockchains, the protocol's leaders can block any misbehaving nodes from the network	
Proof-of-Burn (PoB)	Coin burn	Burn coins to win the right to propose a block	Proposing an invalid block results in wasted time and money	

Source: Kraken Intelligence, CoinGecko
*Note: The market dominance figure for "other" includes tokens, which are cryptoassets built on top of existing L1 blockchains. Tokens do not have their own blockchain and must follow the protocol rules of the chain they operate on.

Figure 2.3 Sybil resistance mechanism overview.

mechanism and a chain selection rule gives us our "consensus method mechanism" (see Figure 2.4).

Interestingly, a key innovation of Bitcoin versus other early crypto-currencies is the invention of the Nakamoto-style consensus mechanism, which relies on proof of work (explained in the next section), created by Satoshi Nakamoto, the inventor of Bitcoin.

This innovation made the network harder to hack, increasing the fault tolerance from 33% to 50%. This helps deter Sybil attacks by increasing the amount of computer power it would require to take control of a network.

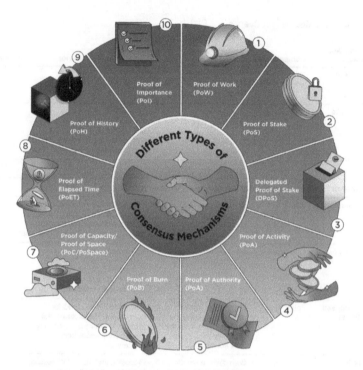

Figure 2.4   Different types of consensus mechanisms.
Source: https://crypto.com/university/consensus-mechanisms-in-blockchain?utm_
source=lnkd&utm_medium=social&utm_campaign=sep10_consensuscharts_lnkd.

Proof of Work

Bitcoin's consensus mechanism is called proof of work (PoW). This method involves nodes competing with each other to solve very complex mathematical problems.

These problems are so large that at present the computer processing speed does not exist for them to be solved in a useful time. This is a hard concept for many to grasp. Understanding the power of mathematics is critical to trusting peer-to-peer digital currencies such as Bitcoin. It is the sheer magnitude of these problems and the amount of time it takes to compute a solution that provides the underlying security.

Once the puzzle has been completed, the miners share their work with other nodes for verification. Once verified in accordance with the consensus mechanism, the new block is added to the chain, and the process repeats.

The core strength of PoW is that it has been tried and tested by Bitcoin for over a decade with no significant security breaches, managing billions of dollars without fail. Remember it is the size of Bitcoin that protects it. The energy required to attempt a 51% hack of the network would be prohibitively expensive. It is worth noting that some smaller PoW blockchains have been successfully hacked. As such, there is a strong argument to be made that it is worth having one very powerful PoW for security, but not all projects should employ PoW consensus mechanisms.

The Proof-of-Work Energy Consumption Debate

A primary criticism of proof-of-work blockchains is their high energy usage. There have been significant concerns raised over the carbon footprint of Bitcoin.

Bitcoin, the world's largest cryptocurrency, currently consumes an estimated 150 terawatt-hours of electricity annually—more than the entire country of Argentina, population 45 million.

Producing that energy emits some 65 megatons of carbon dioxide into the atmosphere annually—comparable to the emissions of Greece.

Recent reports estimate that Bitcoin uses about 0.16% of the global energy demand. While this is in fact a fraction of 1% of the global supply, it is still a significant amount, enough to make it infeasible to expect every blockchain to operate using this consensus mechanism.

With energy being the most significant variable cost in the Bitcoin mining process, miners are incentivized to operate in geographical regions where electricity costs are lower. In the past, this was primarily in subsidized areas of China that operated coal-burning power plants. This of course raised legitimate ecological concerns.

However, in recent years there has been a consistent migration of mining toward renewable energy sources such as those found naturally in countries such as Iceland. In this way, there is a strong argument to be made that it is the space race involved in Bitcoin miners competing to solve the hash algorithms with increasingly faster computers that is

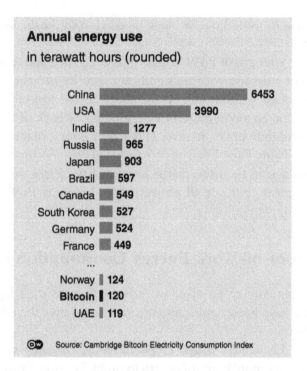

Annual energy use

in terawatt hours (rounded)

China	6453
USA	3990
India	1277
Russia	965
Japan	903
Brazil	597
Canada	549
South Korea	527
Germany	524
France	449
...	
Norway	124
Bitcoin	120
UAE	119

Source: Cambridge Bitcoin Electricity Consumption Index

Figure 2.5   Annual energy use.
Source: https://news.climate.columbia.edu/2022/05/04/cryptocurrency-energy/; https://www.dw.com/en/why-does-bitcoin-need-more-energy-than-whole-countries/a-56573390.

pushing the industry toward a consistently increased reliance on renewables as a percentage of the overall energy supply.

As previously explained, it is not feasible for all blockchains to operate using proof-of-work mining, as the burden on global energy demand would be significant. This is a unique characteristic of Bitcoin given its first mover advantage and wide adoption, and it is likely to remain the underlying security layer for the cryptocurrency sector.

We now have a better understanding of how PoW blockchains like Bitcoin operate, and why it requires a relatively high level of energy use for security, to achieve Sybil resistance. Essentially, this can be summarized as the "nothing at stake problem." If there is no cost to participating in the block validation process then it is easier for bad operators to undertake a large-scale attack.

We mentioned earlier that Quantum computers may be able to corrupt the encryption on an individual node within a useful time frame. However, to corrupt the Bitcoin blockchain a bad operator would have to corrupt over 51% of the nodes before the next block is created.

Currently, for Bitcoin, this happens approximately every ten minutes. The amount of energy needed to control this many nodes is huge. Conversely, the high energy used to maintain the Bitcoin proof-of-work blockchain provides an additional level of security to prevent 51% attacks.

While it may not be the most efficient blockchain for settling transactions or operating smart contracts, Bitcoin is likely to remain a store of value at the center of the cryptocurrency ecosystem, much like gold was before Bretton Woods.

Most cryptocurrency projects that have followed Bitcoin operate a different mining consensus mechanism that is less demanding in terms of energy usage and offers differing degrees of security and functionality.

Proof of Stake

The proof-of-stake consensus mechanism is the most widely adopted model. Instead of using electricity to mine the digital currency, validators simply stake their coins on the network and receive voting power commensurate with the value of their coin holdings.

Validators are selected at random in proportion to the size of their staked holdings of cryptocurrency. The node validates the block, attaches a digital signature, and proposes the block to the network to be added to the blockchain.

As validators are no longer solving complex mathematical problems, there is no longer a need for sophisticated computers that consume a lot of energy. As such, Sybil resistance requires virtually no energy consumption. Due to the low requirement for energy, fewer coins need to be issued to incentivize participation. Validators no longer need costly sophisticated hardware to run mining rigs, eliminating the high cost of entry of new participants.

Proof of Work vs. Proof of Stake

Due to the uncertainty regarding the regulation of digital assets at the time of writing this book, we have chosen to focus primarily on Bitcoin, briefly mention Ethereum, and not name any other cryptocurrency projects. We feel this will also avoid confusion while we are introducing so many new concepts in quick succession.

Above we have introduced both PoW and PoS consensus mechanisms. PoW requires energy to solve complex problems, mine the first block, and receive the reward. PoS requires less energy as it does not require large complex computing operations to mine. A standard device is sufficient for mining as the rewards are distributed based on the stake held by miners. Participants can dedicate their crypto assets to block validators in return for a yield referred to as a staking reward (more on this later).

The different methodologies employed result in different characteristics for the networks, which result in different strengths and concerns. Arguably, PoW is more secure as it discourages forking and is very energy intensive to hack, at least in the case of Bitcoin, as it is well decentralized, with many participating miners. Meanwhile, PoS uses less energy and offers rewards for holders of the network token.

Remember the blockchain trilemma discussed previously; it highlighted the trade-off that exists between scalability, security, and decentralization. Both methods have their limitations. PoW requires a lot of energy and expensive sophisticated computing facilities, a cost that prohibits decentralization as scalability is costly. PoS, on the other hand, is less costly to operate; however, there are often minimum token-holding requirements for node operators, which can act as a barrier to entry. For example, Ethereum requires that an individual who wants to run a node without third-party involvement must stake a minimum sum of 32 ETH. Furthermore, the new tokens and voting rights are generally distributed proportionally to the holdings of tokens, which can lead to a centralization of power that may not be desirable.

We Hate Forking Hackers!

The PoS consensus mechanism uses far less energy than PoW, as it selects validators based on their stake in the underlying ecosystem token.

	Proof-of-work	Proof-of-stake
Mining/validating a block	The amount of computing work determines the probability of mining a block.	The amount of stake, or number of coins, determines the likelihood of validating a new block.
Disribution of reward	The one who mines the block first receives a reward.	The validator does not receive a block reward as they are paid a network fee.
Competition	Miners must compete to solve complex puzzles using their computer processing power.	An algorithm determines a winner based on the size of their stake.
Centralization	PoW solutions are increasingly designated for large-scale operations; they are centralized in nature.	An algorithm determines a winner based on the size of their stake.
Specialized equipment	Application-specific integrated circuits (ASICs) and graphics processing unit (GPUs) are used to mine the coins.	A standard server-grade device is sufficient for PoS-based systems.
Adding a malicious block	To introduce a malicious block, hackers would need 51% of computing power.	Hackers would need to hold 51% of all cryptocurrency on the network.
Efficiency and reliability	PoW systems are less energy-efficient and less expensive, but they are more reliable.	PoS systems are far more cost- and energy-efficient although they are less reliable.
Security	The greater the hash, the more secure the network is.	Staking helps lock crypto assets to secure the network in exchange for a reward.
Forking	Through an economic incentive, PoW systems naturally prevent constant forking.	Forking is not automatically discouraged by PoS systems.

Figure 2.6 Proof-of-work vs. proof-of-stake: Pros, cons, and differences explained. Source: https://cointelegraph.com/blockchain-for-beginners/proof-of-stake-vs-proof-of-work:-differences-explained / Cointelegraph / last accessed Aug 26, 2023.

While this may be more environmentally friendly concerning energy demand, it also has some shortcomings.

When changes are made to the rules that define how a blockchain protocol works, the community splits the chain. A copy is made of the original chain in a process referred to as "forking." Then the majority of the community will migrate operations to the new fork with the updated set of rules.

There are two types of forks. A "soft fork" is like a software upgrade for adding new functions and features. It is backward-compatible with the existing blockchain or pre-fork blocks. So, after the changes are made there is still a single blockchain.

Meanwhile a "hard fork" involves structural changes to the underlying code that are not compatible with the existing blockchain. As such a "fork" is made of the chain, the agreed changes are applied, and the community moves to the new chain—essentially a new cryptocurrency is born, or perhaps "spawned" is a more accurate description.

Remember our multiple personality disorder patient Sybil. With PoW, hackers are deterred from creating scale attacks due to the energy cost of undertaking such attacks. However, with PoS blockchains, if the cost of attack is not high enough, then it is possible to try and fork a blockchain for numerous nefarious activities. This stimulates bribery and collusion among dishonest validators.

This low cost of corruption can lead to the nothing-at-stake problem, where a validator accepts both forks to try and earn double rewards. Another concern is "selfish mining attacks," which involve miners colluding to withhold a block from the blockchain and then creating a fork that results in a longer chain than the original. With Nakamoto-style consensus, this new longer chain with false data allows hackers to steal or double-spend the underlying token.

It is logical to assume that lower transaction ("gas") fees are always better. However, zero or very low fees make it easier for bad operators to send junk data to execute DDoS attacks, for example. Similarly, fees promote competition between operators, which helps to avoid collusion and network hacks.

This is an important consideration when selecting which blockchain to use. Lower transaction fees are beneficial from a cost consideration, but if fees are too low and the blockchain is not suitably diversified, the result may be a low cost of attack, which will attract nefarious operators.

Don't worry! Not everyone is out to get you. The underlying ethos of blockchain technology is transparency and collaboration. Miners earn the underlying coin in the network, they earn a living from the network, and as such, they are incentivized to protect it.

Staking Rewards

Participants in PoS blockchains can contribute their tokens to the network to earn a percentage return on the value of their assets. This can take several forms, but to oversimplify, it is akin to depositing money at a traditional bank and earning a rate of interest on the principal sum.

Unfortunately, just like with the fiat banking system, you have little knowledge or control over the risks that could affect the institution or network in the case of cryptocurrency, which could place not just your proposed yield earnings at risk but could lead to the loss of your entire investment.

The yield or rate of return depends on several factors. In its simplest form, if staking directly with the network, the yield should be determined based on the number of rewards to be released over the staking window (or lockup period), divided among the participants who are staking.

This last point is very important! To reiterate, the total amount to be distributed is divided among the token holders that decide to stake for rewards. This has two significant outcomes. The first key outcome is that if you are staking your tokens in a network that would yield 10% per year with 100% participation and the current participation rate is only 50%, then the return for those staking jumps to 20% per year. The second key outcome concerning PoW staking rewards is that if you hold the token but are not actively delegating your stake to earn yield, then the value of your holding is being inflated away, exactly like fiat currency subject to the money printing of central banks. Remember that most PoW crypto tokens are not fixed in supply like Bitcoin.

This means that if you are holding PoW tokens and you are not staking for yield, your holding is losing value as the total supply grows as staking rewards are issued. Over time, the compounding effect of not staking in the face of growing supply can have a significant impact on long-term returns.

Next, we will have a look at the Ethereum network and how it is transitioning from a PoW blockchain to PoS in an event that has become known as "the merge."

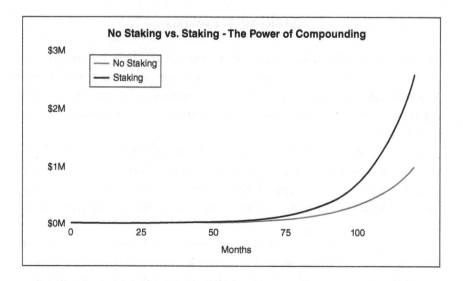

Figure 2.7 No staking vs. staking—the power of compounding.
Source: Stakingrewards.com.

Merge Right to Avoid Danger Ahead!

To avoid confusion, this book will focus almost solely on Bitcoin as we discuss the topic of cryptocurrency trading. However, to illuminate the topic of consensus mechanism selection, it would be remiss not to mention Ethereum.

Ethereum was founded as a more functional alternative to Bitcoin, which is designed to operate as a digital currency. Ethereum is a development platform that allows for more detailed contracts and projects to be created. While books could (and have) been written about Ethereum, this will not be another one.

Bitcoin vs. Ethereum

	Bitcoin	Ethereum
Creator(s)	Satoshi Nakamoto	Vitalik Buterin, Charles Hoskinson, Gavin Wood, Jeffrey Wilcke, Mihai Alisie, Anthony Di Iorio, and Amir Chetrit
Launch date	January 2009	July 2015
Currency vs. platform	A credible alternative to traditional fiat currencies (medium of exchange, store of value)	A platform to run programmatic contracts and applications via Ether
Consensus algorithm	Proof-of-Work	Proof-of-Work, moving to Proof-of-Stake
Block time	10 minutes on average	15 seconds on average
Transaction throughput	7 transactions per second	30 transactions per second
Supply	Finite supply, capped at 21 million BTC	Infinite supply

Figure 2.8 Bitcoin vs. Ethereum.
Source: https://cointelegraph.com/ethereum-for-beginners/bitcoin-vs-ethereum-key-differences-between-btc-and-eth.

Ethereum must be mentioned as, after Bitcoin, it is, without doubt, the most powerful cryptocurrency project. At the time of writing, the market capitalization of Ethereum is one-third that of Bitcoin. Many believe that it could converge and outgrow Bitcoin in coming years as the cryptocurrency markets develop and more global commerce takes place on-chain. At present, should the merge prove successful over time, it should cement Ethereum as the dominant functional blockchain globally.

Interestingly, Ethereum completed the transition from a proof-of-work (PoW) to a proof-of-stake (PoS) consensus mechanism. What does this all mean, and how does it change Ethereum from an investment perspective?

Most blockchains actually operate a proof-of-stake consensus mechanism. Remember with PoS, the rewards and voting power are distributed based on the amount of the underlying token one holds.

The Ethereum 2.0 merge involves a series of updates designed to transition the blockchain from PoW to PoS. This will immediately lower the energy usage of the blockchain by about 99%. While PoW mining involves expensive cutting-edge hardware and large amounts of energy, PoS mining can be performed on a regular laptop as it does not require the solving of large problems by fast processors or graphics cards.

So while the move from PoW to PoS lowers the energy usage of Ethereum, it may actually decrease the level of decentralization of the network. To operate an Ethereum blockchain node will require validators to hold a minimum 32 ETH. This creates a financial barrier to entry for miners to join the network, potentially affecting scalability and dissuading decentralization.

Interestingly, it is the level of decentralization of the Ethereum network that is likely to see it regulated as a currency and not a security. Could this migration from PoW to PoS decrease the level of decentralization, which could jeopardize Ethereum's currency classification by the US Commodity Futures Trading Commission (CFTC)?

If Ethereum were to be investigated by the SEC and potentially be classified as a security instead of a currency, this would have serious implications for its value. However, at present, it looks as though Bitcoin and Ethereum are set to be blessed by the CFTC as currencies, which would see huge inflows of capital to ETH and BTC futures contracts and would likely drive prices higher from current low levels.

For Ethereum, having managed to navigate the complicated path to PoS, the holy grail is the ability for it to offer "staking rewards" to holders of the cryptocurrency. Bitcoin mining does not allow holders of Bitcoin to earn a yield on their holdings directly from the network.

Staking rewards enable holders of the cryptocurrency to designate their crypto to a mining operator and earn a yield on their holdings. The ideal situation for Ethereum would be if it manages the complicated technological task of migrating to proof of stake and maintains its classification as a currency and not security by US regulators.

A successful transition from PoW to PoS mining merge has long-term bullish implications for Ethereum. The reduction in energy usage reduces costs for validators and improves their carbon footprint, an important factor for ESG-led investors. The contraction in supply, and the ability to earn staking rewards, should be a strong driver of future value.

Stable Coins and CBDCs

"Stable coins," or perhaps "fiat-pegged tokens," may be a better term to describe how current real-world currencies are adapted to operate in the cryptocurrency ecosystem. In the early development of cryptocurrency trading, investors needed a way to transact against the value of the US dollar without converting crypto investments back to fiat currency constantly. The borderless and unregulated nature of cryptocurrency exchanges meant participants wanted to avoid interacting with the fiat monetary system.

This gave rise to a class of investment tokens that were in theory identical to the underlying currency, most commonly the US dollar, the idea being that one dollar of a "stable" US dollar coin was redeemable for one US dollar of paper money. However, in practice this has not always been the case. Audits of major stable coins treasuries showed that they were more like hedge funds under the hood.

The collapse of Terra Luna, which was an algorithmic fiat-pegged coin, sent shockwaves through the cryptocurrency sector, resulting in widespread losses in the tens of billions. This collapse along with other market manipulation cases highlight the urgent need for regulation in the space.

Governments have taken notice and global regulation is likely to be announced in the coming months. I imagine by the time you are reading this, regulations will likely be in place. Regulation is just one step to be implemented by governments. The benefits of digital currencies have not gone unnoticed by governments, who are already working with the traditional banking sector to move the world toward a cashless economy.

In time, governments will step in with their own cryptocurrencies, which are referred to as Central Bank Digital Currencies (CBDCs). We will not dwell on CBDCs or stablecoins. They do deserve research and need to be understood. They offer no return, so investors are taking an uncompensated risk when they use them.

In the next chapter, we will discuss methods of valuing Bitcoin. Then we will move on to price charts and technical analysis to help you develop a tool set so you can analyze the price movements of your crypto holdings.

Chapter 3

Valuing Bitcoin

"A fool is someone who knows the price of everything and the value
of nothing."

—*Oscar Wilde*

To Own Crypto Is to Understand Crypto

A common barrier for investors to start investing in cryptocurrency is
that they do not understand enough about it. Hopefully, this book will
help in this process! Investors fear the big first leap—that first purchase.

The advice is always the same. To get started, why not buy $10 of
Bitcoin? To do this one must open a wallet and purchase some Bitcoin.
This exercise alone has a reasonable learning curve. As investors grow
their knowledge, they become more comfortable with cryptocurrency
and usually start to read more on the topic.

Since its inception, there has been a wide range of estimates for
the potential value of Bitcoin. While skeptics believe it will collapse

to zero, many Bitcoin evangelists have employed a variety of analysis techniques to estimate the potential value of Bitcoin as adoption increases.

So let's take a look at some of the models that have gained notoriety over time. It seems fitting that the first valuation that we assess is that of none other than Satoshi.

So How Much Could One Bitcoin Eventually Be Worth?

In early emails between the creator of Bitcoin, Satoshi Nakamoto, and Hal Finney (the recipient of the first-ever Bitcoin transaction), a future potential price of $10 million per Bitcoin was discussed (Bitcoin is currently trading at approximately $28,000 as of July 2023). Hal Finney based this valuation on an assumption that Bitcoin would become the world's underlying payment system. See the email below where he asks Satoshi:

> Do you think this could scale to be usable for close to 100% of world financial transactions?

Hal Finney's Ambitious Bitcoin Valuation

One may conclude that to arrive at his $10 million valuation he was dividing the total value of the global monetary supply by the total supply of Bitcoin, which is fixed at 21 million coins. Given that this email exchange took place in 2008, before the launch of Bitcoin, the value of the global monetary system has increased by multiples, which means that Hal Finney's price target is far too low given his rationale.

Finney is on the record as claiming that if Bitcoin does achieve the target of becoming the core of global financial transactions, then a price could be almost limitless, stating that Bitcoin:

> Should be equal to the total value of all the wealth in the world.

```
From hal@finney.org  Wed Nov 19 07:20:46 2008
Return-Path: <hal@finney.org>
X-Original-To: hal@finney.org
Delivered-To: hal@finney.org
Received: by finney.org (Postfix, from userid 500)
        id A78D414F6E2; Wed, 19 Nov 2008 07:20:46 -0800 (PST)
To: hal@finney.org, satoshi@vistomail.com
Subject: Re: Bitcoin source files attached
Cc: bear@sonic.net, jamesd@echeque.com
Message-Id: <20081119152046.A78D414F6E2@finney.org>
Date: Wed, 19 Nov 2008 07:20:46 -0800 (PST)
From: hal@finney.org ("Hal Finney")
X-Bogosity: Ham, tests=bogofilter, spamicity=0.000000, version=1.0.3
Status: RO

Ah, I see, thanks for the corrections.

Some of the discussion and concern over performance may relate to the
eventual size of the P2P node network. How large do you envision it
becoming? Tens of nodes? Thousands?  Millions?

And for clients, do you think this could scale to be usable for close
to 100% of world financial transactions? Or would you see it as mostly
being used for some "core" subset of transactions that have special
requirements, with other transactions using a different payment system
that perhaps is based on Bitcoin?

Hal
```

Figure 3.1 Previously unpublished emails of Satoshi Nakamoto present a new puzzle.
Source: CoinDesk / https://www.coindesk.com/markets/2020/11/26/previously-unpublished-emailsof-satoshi-nakamoto-present-a-new-puzzle/Last preview on 19. Feb 2024.

An ambitious price target to say the least! It seems fitting that the first valuation that we assessed was linked directly to conversations with Satoshi. So let's take a look at some of the other valuation models that have gained notoriety over time.

Hal Finney arrived at a lofty valuation for a single Bitcoin by assuming that Bitcoin would be equal to the value of the entire global financial system. This is potentially a little too optimistic, but time will tell.

There is a multitude of creative methods for calculating a future potential valuation for Bitcoin: techniques that analyze trading volumes, some that compare it to other investment asset classes, and others that rely on a complex analysis of transaction data. Let's have a look at some of the other valuation methodologies that have been employed.

Bitcoin as Digital Gold

Bitcoin has been compared to gold since the beginning of its existence. They share many key characteristics that make both potentially very good stores of value. Both exhibit portability across international boundaries, global acceptance in exchange for local currencies, and can be transferred peer-to-peer with no intermediary.

They do have some notable differences, which are also worth considering when deciding their value as investments. For example, it is a lot easier to carry $1 billion of Bitcoin versus $1 billion of physical gold bullion.

Limited supply is a key characteristic that sees Bitcoin compared to gold as opposed to traditional fiat currencies such as the US dollar. The total supply of gold is estimated to be relatively finite, which constrains supply. Furthermore, the cost of mining puts a floor in the value of the commodity.

When the price drops too low, miners will stop working, as it costs more to extract the gold. This in turn tightens the supply of gold in the market, which helps to stabilize prices.

The supply of Bitcoin is fixed at 21 million, making it relatively unique among currencies, especially the fiat kind. Most cryptocurrencies and tokens do not have fixed supplies either. It is this characteristic of Bitcoin that leads to the comparison with gold.

The fixed supply prevents governments or central banks from printing more to serve their purposes. By structurally preventing debasement, Bitcoin ensures that its value will not be eroded by excessive money printing. This is a topic we have discussed previously in more detail. This characteristic makes it very attractive to libertarians, who believe money and the state should be separated.

Bitcoin's Production Value

Bitcoin is a proof-of-work blockchain. We discussed this in detail in the previous section on how Bitcoin works. Remember that rewards are distributed to miners who apply sophisticated computers to solve complex mathematical problems (hash equations). As such the overall power of the network is measured in what is referred to as the "hash rate."

The Bitcoin blockchain requires a significant amount of energy to run the mining rig computers. As such, this energy consumption is the cost of

Figure 3.2   Bitcoin's production value.

mining Bitcoin. A clear comparison can be drawn by miners between the cost to them of mining a Bitcoin and the current market price of a Bitcoin (or expected present value, to be more precise).

The Bitcoin Hash Rate

The Bitcoin network operates a proof-of-work consensus method that requires miners to solve complex equations with powerful multi-processor computers. The combined effort of all these miners working together gives us the hash rate.

The higher the hash rate, the faster and more secure the network. There is a strong positive correlation between Bitcoin prices and its hash rate. This is logical, as a higher price will attract more and increasingly sophisticated miners.

Value as a Multiple of Mining Cost

Should it cost more to mine a Bitcoin than they could sell it for, it would make no sense for a miner to continue to do so. If they are no longer earning a profit, the relatively inefficient miners will leave the market to be replaced by miners with better technology and/or cheaper electricity costs that afford them a better profitability ratio.

Figure 3.4 below shows the miner profitability ratio of Bitcoin over time compared to the price of Bitcoin. When the ratio is below zero it

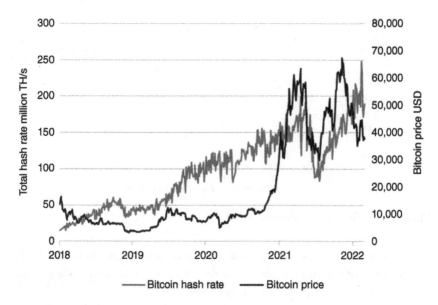

Figure 3.3 Image: Bitcoin hash rate vs. bitcoin price.
Source: on-chain data from blockchain.com, price data from coinmarketcap.com.

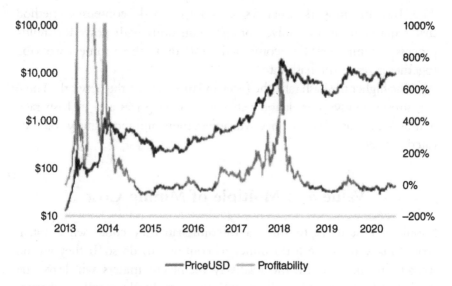

Figure 3.4 Miner profitability ratio.

means it is unprofitable for miners to operate. It is worth noting these have proven to be good long-term buying opportunities.

Paul Tudor Jones, whose concerns over monetary debasement we mentioned in Chapter 1, has created a model for analyzing the value of different economic stores of value in times of inflation. He outlines four criteria on which investments would be ranked between one and one hundred. They are: power, trustworthiness, liquidity, and portability.

	Purchasing Power*	Trust*	Liquidity*	Portability*	Total Score	Market Capitalization ($ millions)
Financial Assets	90	65	60	60	71	$266,917,000
Cash	5	60	90	80	54	$39,000,000
Gold	70	85	45	30	62	$11,938,404
Bitcoin	50	5	50	80	43	$207,283

Figure 3.5 Paul Tudor Jones store of value scoring as of August 4, 2020.

Comparing financial assets, cash, gold, and Bitcoin, Jones awarded Bitcoin the lowest overall score. However, the mere fact that it was in the same ballpark as the other asset classes got Jones's attention.

> What was surprising to me was not that Bitcoin came in last, but that it scored as high as it did. Bitcoin had an overall score nearly 60% of that of financial assets but has a market cap that is 1/1200th of that. It scores 66% of gold as a store of value, but has a market cap that is 1/60th of gold's outstanding value. Something appears wrong here and my guess is it is the price of Bitcoin.

The real potential driver for upside was revealed when comparing the total market capitalization of the investments. With Bitcoin so far behind in value yet reasonably close in utility, a convergence to the mean generates significant upside targets for the future market capitalization of Bitcoin.

Relative Valuation

A very common practice across investing asset classes is the concept of relative valuation, comparing the total value of one asset to another. In this instance, we will analyze the total value of different investment asset classes and compare them to the total market cap of Bitcoin (or the entire crypto-investible universe).

Given the total supply of Bitcoin is fixed and the current mined supply is known, it is straightforward to calculate the total market capitalization for Bitcoin. In reality, the active supply of Bitcoin is very different from the total supply, as many coins have been lost forever or are sitting in inactive wallets, while others have been blacklisted and frozen.

When we see how the value of the entire crypto market compares to other asset classes, it is clear there is still considerable potential upside. If all money and stock market value were to move to the cryptocurrency sector, the entire market could see an astronomical move from current levels. Now, some may consider this unlikely, but every year it becomes a little more possible.

Asset Class	Size ($trn)	Asset Class	Size ($trn)
Bonds	129.0	Crypto	1.3
... Government	88.0	... Bitcoin	0.6
... Corporate	41.0	... Ether	0.2
Equity	88.0	USD M2	22.0
... Developed	66.0	... Notes & Coins	2.2
... Emerging	22.0	EUR M2	16.4
Private Markets	6.5	... Notes & Coins	2.1
... PE & VC	3.8	JPY M2	9.6
... Private Debt	0.9	... Notes & Coins	1.0
... Real Estate	1.0	GBP M2	3.9
... Infrastructure	0.8	... Notes & Coins	0.1
Gold	16.0		
Silver	1.5		

Exhibit 3.1 Asset class value and money as of February 2022.
Source: "An Investor's Guide to Crypto," Campbell R. Harvey, Tarek Abou Zeid, Teun Draaisma, Martin Luk, Henry Neville, Andre Rzym, and Otto van Hemert, version: June 1, 2022.

Perhaps a more realistic comparison that has long been touted in the media is that Bitcoin is the new "digital gold." An unleveraged store of value that can sit at the base of the money system acts as a store of value

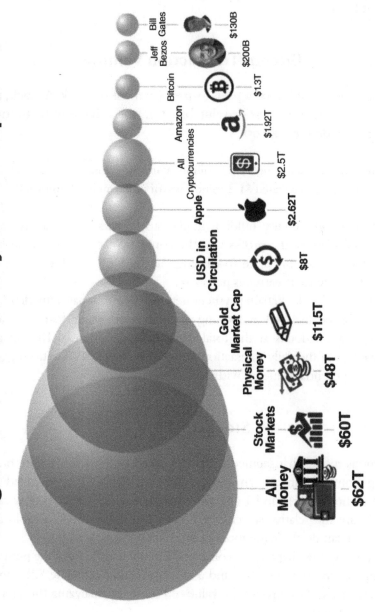

Figure 3.6 Putting the world's money into perspective.

Source: Adapted from https://howmuch.net/articles/worlds-money-in-perspective-2018 with updated 2024 data from Google Finance, TradingView, and https://www.visualcapitalist.com.

against which other assets can be priced. If the market capitalization of gold investment is roughly $8 trillion, then that is still a 20× increase from current levels.

Bitcoin Transaction Volume

Bitcoin was created to be a peer-to-peer payment network. As such, it is logical to judge its success or value based on the volume of transactions taking place on the network.

> Bitcoin recorded roughly $2 trillion worth of transactions in 2021, while PayPal facilitated $1.2 trillion worth of payments. (Finimize)

A traditional equity holding in the stock market pays a dividend, which is a share of the profits that the company earns. As such, analysts value companies using price-to-earnings ratios (P/E), which compare the price of a share to its earnings per share.

However, a blockchain payment network does not pay a dividend. As such, it can be analyzed by looking at the network-value-to-transactions (NVT) ratio. It looks at the total market capitalization of Bitcoin and compares it to the daily transaction volume. A lower NVT ratio suggests increased potential value, as with a stock PE ratio.

Stock-to-Flow

A famous model that seemed to have worked well for some time but is fading from relevance is an extrapolation of the NVT ratio called the stock-to-flow (S2F) model or ratio. Analysts use the stock-to-flow ratio to measure the relative scarcity of finite commodities such as gold and silver. You can do the same for Bitcoin.

Earlier in this chapter, we compared Bitcoin to gold from the perspective of scarcity, mining costs, and asset class market cap. The S2F model has been derived to forecast the value of Bitcoin by analyzing the supply-side value drivers.

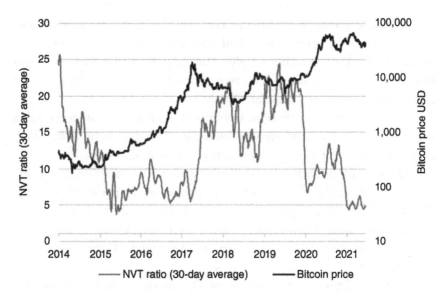

Figure 3.7 NVT ratio vs. Bitcoin price.
Source: on-chain data from blockchain.com, price data from coinmarketcap.com.

Using the concept of looking at the overall market capitalization of Bitcoin versus the value transacted over time gives us a measure of value similar to stock price–earnings ratios.

The S2F model divides Bitcoin into two categories: the "stock" of Bitcoin refers to the total supply that has already been mined and is available in the market (in theory), and the "flow" of Bitcoin refers to the new supply that has been added by mining in the past 12 months.

Stock to Flow of Bitcoin, Gold and Silver				
Asset	**Total Supply**	**Annual Increase**	**Stock-to-Flow Ratio**	**Annual Supply Growth**
Bitcoin	19,171,050	328,500	58.3	1.6%
Gold	187,000 tons	3,000	62.3	1.7%
Silver	550,000 tons	25,000	22	4.5%

Figure 3.8 Stock to flow of Bitcoin, gold, and silver.
Source: *Forbes* https://www.forbes.com/advisor/investing/cryptocurrency/bitcoin-stock-to-flow-model/.

The table above highlights the stock-to-flow ratios of Bitcoin compared to gold and silver. The calculation divides the annual increase in supply by the total available supply. This gives us a ratio that represents how many years of mining at current production levels would it take to replace the current total available supply.

The ratio represents years, so from the table above we can deduce that it would take 58.3 years to replace Bitcoin stock with current flow, which is very similar to the stock-to-flow ratio of gold at 62.3 years.

The scarcity provided by Bitcoin's fixed supply means that its value cannot be debased like the US dollar through central bank money printing. The final total supply figure is known and fixed at 21 million. We can estimate how long this will take to mine over time, giving us a dynamic model, which allows us to project a growth forecast for Bitcoin prices into the future.

Visual analysis of the overlay of the model forecast versus Bitcoin is very impressive to date. However, as all disclaimers say, "Past performance is not an accurate indication of future price performance." Some of the visual correlation may be coincidental here, meaning it worked for a while but coincidentally, as opposed to having any real prediction value.

At the time of writing, the model suggests Bitcoin should be trading at over 100 thousand dollars, instead, as of this writing, it's trading about $26,000. Furthermore, as the Bitcoin mining algorithm will become increasingly stingy over time, the model pricing will become exponential toward the end of the minting cycle, which would suggest some astronomical price predictions.

A damning analysis of the methodology by Ethereum founder Vitalik Buterin highlights the current failings of the model. In the next section, we look at another model that may offer a better future prediction for the trajectory of Bitcoin prices.

Metcalf's Law

Cryptocurrencies are based on blockchains, which are essentially networks of users. We have already looked at increases in active wallet addresses as an indicator of the strength of Bitcoin growth.

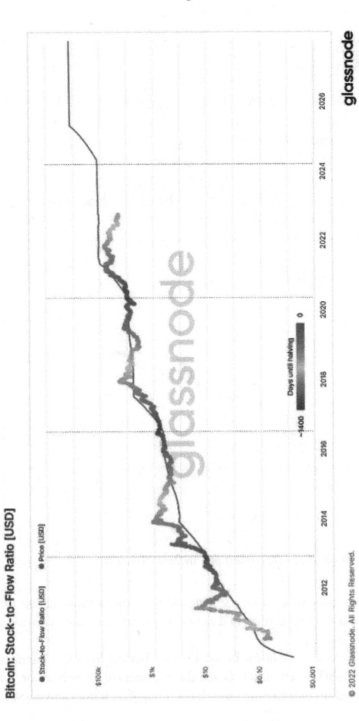

Figure 3.9 Bitcoin stock-to-flow ratio.

Stock-to-flow is really not looking good now.

I know it's impolite to gloat and all that, but I think financial models that give people a false sense of certainty and predestination that number-will-go-up are harmful and deserve all the mockery they get.

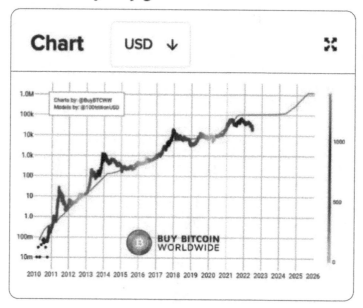

Figure 3.10 X (formerly Twitter) post by Vitalik Buterin.

The thesis goes, more active wallet addresses mean more active users, which should result in increased network activity and value creation (all else being equal).

Networks are not linear in nature; they benefit from the interaction of the nodes with each other. Given this exponential growth factor, what is a good way to measure the growth potential of such interactive systems?

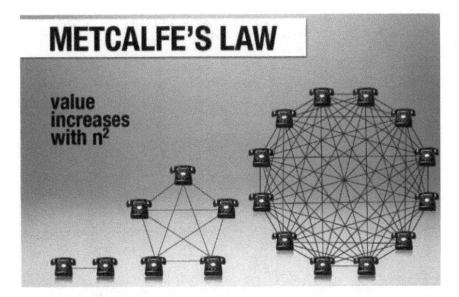

Figure 3.11   Metcalf's law.
Source: https://www.inbitcoinwetrust.net/bitcoin-will-remain-the-undisputed-cryptocurrencies-leader-for-a-long-time-5b97513af3e8.

The underlying concept of Metcalfe's law was originally introduced by George Gilder to describe the growth of communications networks. The formula was later adapted to describe the growth of Ethernet by Robert Metcalfe, after whom the law is named.

A common example given to explain the premise is that of the fax machine. A single fax machine has no value, as there is nobody to receive the communication. However, the value of owning a fax machine increases as more participants join the network, expanding the scope for interaction between participants.

Metcalf's law states that the value of a network is proportional to the number of connected users squared, or n^2, where n is the number of participants. As such, the growth of such networks can be described as exponential (or asymptotic, to be precise).

In more recent times, Metcalf's law has been used to describe user growth of tech companies, social media networks, and the Internet itself. The chart in Figure 3.12 shows the growth of Bitcoin users (wallets) versus the Internet. Notice how Bitcoin is growing at a faster rate, making

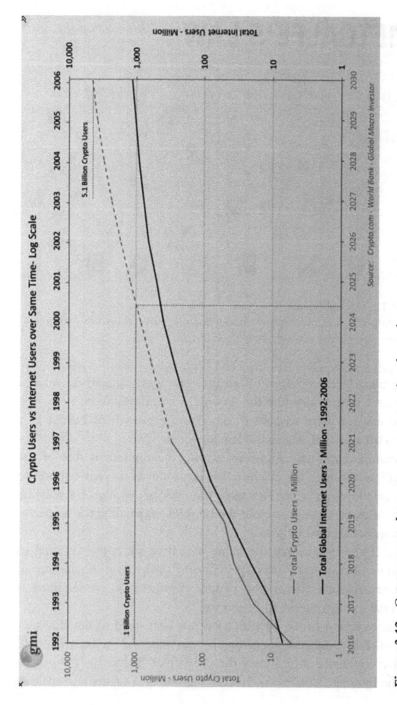

Figure 3.12 Crypto users vs. Internet users over same time; log scale.
Source: https://twitter.com/RaoulGMI/status/1502638102002782213/photo/1.

it perhaps the most impressive uptake of technology in recorded human history—data on the adoption rate of "the wheel" is a little unreliable!

There have also been some questions over the reliability of the data used for Bitcoin, with many believing that the number of wallet addresses is overstated as individuals can and often do have multiple wallets.

Active wallet addresses are a better measure than total wallet addresses. The average activity of each transaction or wallet over time could also be used to assess the data more accurately. As long as we are then comparing apples to apples over time, the magnitude of growth should reflect the network effect.

A more damning assessment was made by Makarov and Schoar (2022), who suggested that Bitcoin users often create new addresses for each transaction. The recent enforcement of KYC (know-your-client) regulations is restricting such practices. Major crypto exchanges now require photographic ID and proof of address for users to operate wallets on their platforms. As this trend continues, the data will become more reliable, as users are tied to fewer addresses that can be linked back to them.

However, it will make comparisons to the past less reliable. As with many of the valuation techniques outlined in this section, the rapidly changing ecosystem and volatile price swings in recent years make it hard to pin down a flawless model that can derive a future value of Bitcoin with a strong degree of accuracy. However, monitoring changes in these models may be useful to predict changes in the price trends of Bitcoin and other cryptocurrencies.

From Long-term Predictions to Short-term Trading

Above, we have reviewed a wide variety of future value prediction techniques, which have returned potential values of Bitcoin from zero to seven figures for a single coin. A clear value at a defined point in time is very hard to predict due to the large number of variables that affect market price moves.

We can conclude the consensus is that if Bitcoin avoids going to zero, it has significant future upside price potential in the coming years, especially if network adoption continues at such astronomical rates.

The timing of such moves has proven difficult to date and is likely to continue to be so. This has not stopped millions from trying their hand at timing the price movements of Bitcoin for profit. While active management does increase profit potential, which can be increased dramatically using borrowing, referred to as leveraged trading, it is not a hobby.

Trading, especially with the use of leverage, significantly increases the risk of losing some or all of your capital in a short space of time. The risk is to be respected! Strategies should be adapted to try and identify, mitigate, and avoid risk as effectively as possible.

In the following sections, we will focus more on active management techniques for trading Bitcoin as opposed to just buying it and storing it. Welcome to the dark arts of technical analysis and quant trading.

Chapter 4

Price Analysis
for Prediction

"History doesn't repeat itself, but it does rhyme."

—Mark Twain

The focus of this book thus far has been understanding the technology that underlies cryptocurrencies and analyzing ways to value these networks. Models are great in principle; it is important to analyze investments using different methodologies to determine a value in practice. This section will focus on time-proven methods to analyze prices to identify trends and key price levels.

The price of an asset is out of your control. Market prices are not determined through a democratic process: each trader is not asked to vote on what their analyzed value is. The players with the most money, the whales, move prices.

Price is where all ideas meet and are judged in real time. It only takes one trader with the opposite opinion and the same amount of capital to negate your impact on the market you are trading. Every time you sell, someone is buying and vice versa. This should remind you that no matter how certain you are in your analysis, there are professionals who hold the exact opposite view at the same time.

Market information is not asymmetric, meaning it is not the same for all participants. When George Soros decides to sell his gold holdings or Elon Musk decides to dump his Bitcoin, unfortunately, they do not tell us first. They place their trade; the impact is seen on prices, and later the information is revealed. Prices move first, and then the reasons why are revealed later. Prices move faster than information. Just as lightning proceeds thunder, sharp price movements often give real-time warnings of important market information that is not yet widely disseminated.

During an extended buy-and-hold bull market, everyone is an expert. All you have to do is buy for any reason, and it goes higher. You are proven correct. This positive feedback loop of higher prices confirming bullish sentiment fuels large market trends. With cryptocurrencies, there is not as much fundamental data as with traditional markets. As such, price action is even more important, and trends are more pronounced. With technical analysis, one can track the mood of the market by closely following the trends in the price action.

The Saga of Investors

Human emotion is the enemy of traders. When the market is going up, everyone is a genius! When the market falls, it is "irrational," or some external event is to blame. The market is designed to play on traders' emotions: fear, greed, and hope drive market participants to make bad decisions.

Successful professionals respect market prices and develop methodologies to analyze the price action, developing a strategy with an edge. An edge may be gained from access to better information. When analyzing price action there are techniques that can be applied to classify market conditions and determine optimal times to trade.

Over the next few chapters, we are going to discuss techniques for analyzing past prices to develop strategies that show a statistical performance edge. As all financial disclaimers highlight, past performance is not an indication of future performance. However, it is definitely preferable to no past analysis at all.

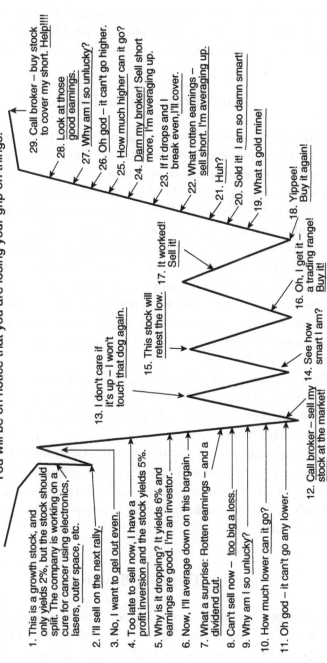

Figure 4.1   The saga of an investor.

There is empirical statistical evidence to suggest the existence of cycles and trends in prices. Our goal is to develop signals and strategies to identify such conditions so we can earn a profit by participating in trends when they arise while avoiding periods of extreme downside volatility.

Are Market Prices Random?

The concept of a random walk suggests that the price movements of a security are random and unpredictable, and therefore it is not possible to consistently outperform the market through technical analysis or other means. This idea is based on the efficient market hypothesis, which states that prices fully reflect all available information and that it is impossible to consistently achieve returns above the market average.

On the other hand, some market participants believe that trends exist in financial markets and that it is possible to identify and follow these trends in order to achieve superior returns. Mean reversion is a market hypothesis that suggests that prices and returns eventually move back toward the mean, or average. This can be thought of as a form of trend-following, as the trader is attempting to identify deviations from the mean and bet on a return toward the average.

Extrapolation is the process of projecting trends or patterns into the future. It is based on the idea that past performance can be used to predict future performance and is often used by traders and investors to try to forecast market movements.

It is important to note that the efficient market hypothesis is not universally accepted, and there is ongoing debate among market participants about the degree to which financial markets are efficient and the extent to which technical analysis and other strategies can be used to achieve superior returns.

Trend Following

Isaac Newton's laws of motion, which describe the relationship between a body and the forces acting upon it, can also be applied to financial markets and the concept of trend following. In particular, Newton's first law states that an object in motion tends to stay in motion, and an object at rest tends to stay at rest. This principle can be applied to trends in the financial markets, as a trending market is likely to continue in the same direction until a significant force acts to change the trend.

This force could be a change in market fundamentals, such as a shift in economic conditions or a change in company earnings, or it could be a technical trigger, such as a breakout from a chart pattern. By following trends and being attuned to potential forces that may change the direction of the trend, traders can potentially capture profits in the financial markets.

Trend following is a popular strategy in the financial markets, especially in trading futures contracts. The idea behind trend following is to identify the overall direction of the market and then to trade in that direction. To do this, traders typically use technical analysis tools such as moving averages and chart patterns to identify trends.

There are several advantages to using trend following as a trading strategy. First, it can be applied to a wide range of financial instruments, including stocks, bonds, commodities, and currencies. Second, it can be used in both bull and bear markets, as the trader is simply looking to follow the direction of the trend rather than trying to predict market tops or bottoms.

One of the main drawbacks of trend following is that it can be difficult to identify trends in the early stages, which can lead to missed opportunities; this is where chart reading may become more of an art than an exact science.

Dow Theory

Charles Dow, the cofounder of Dow Jones & Company and creator of the Dow Jones Industrial Average (DJIA), believed that the stock market was a leading indicator of the overall health of the economy. Dow theory was formulated from a series of *Wall Street Journal* editorials authored by Charles Dow from 1900 until the time of his death in 1902.

Dow theory uses stock price movement and trends to understand and forecast market behavior. He believed that by analyzing the overall market and individual stocks, investors could identify trends and make informed decisions about where to invest their money. The six tenets of Dow theory are outlined below. We will discuss these in more detail as they serve as a solid basis for understanding market price analysis for the prediction of future trends.

1. The Averages Discount Everything

Dow believed that stock prices reflect all available information about a company and its prospects, including economic, political, and social factors. This means that stock prices should fully reflect the underlying business conditions and trends and that by analyzing stock prices, one can gain insight into the overall market and the economy.

The price is updated in real time and so reflects the actions taken by all market participants. Prices move faster than information. Unfortunately, as mentioned above, George Soros doesn't warn the world before he sells his gold holdings. He sells, the price moves, and then later, in regulatory filings, the information is disseminated. Price creation is not elected democratically; the big players with the most money have the biggest impact on price movements.

Price is the one piece of information that all traders and investors receive at the same time. There is a beautiful equality to the study of price action. The price is never wrong! It is a trader's job to stay on the right side of the trend.

2. The Market Has Three Trends

Dow theory identifies three trends in the market: the primary trend, the intermediate trend, and the short-term trend. The primary trend is the long-term direction of the market, which can last for several years. The intermediate trend is the medium-term direction of the market, which can last for several months. The short-term trend is the direction of the market over a period of weeks or days.

Regardless of trend length, the primary trend remains in effect until there is a confirmed reversal. A secondary trend moves in the opposite direction of the primary trend, or as a correction to the primary trend. For example, an upward primary trend will be composed of secondary downward trends and vice versa. The retracement of the secondary trend generally ranges between one-third to two-thirds of the primary trend's movement. In general, a secondary, or intermediate, trend typically lasts between three weeks and three months. The last of the three trend types in Dow theory is the minor trend, which is defined as a market movement lasting less than three weeks.

Charles Dow had a wonderful analogy for analyzing price action. He compared prices to the ocean. The ocean is one body of water where you have different cycles of varying magnitudes: the tide, the wave, the ripple.

Dow used this metaphor to explain the interaction of the primary, intermediate, and short-term price trends. Just as the tide is more significant than a wave and ripple, Dow advised that market analysts should give more significance to the long-term trends.

3. Major Trends Have Three Phases

Dow theory posits that major trends go through three phases: an accumulation phase, a public participation phase, and a distribution phase.

During the accumulation phase, professional investors and insiders buy up large quantities of stocks, often at discounted prices. Next comes the public participation phase: the general public becomes aware of the trend and begins to buy into the market, driving prices up.

When informed investors entered the market during the accumulation phase, they did so with the assumption that the worst was over and a recovery lay ahead. As this starts to materialize, the new primary trend moves into the second phase, the public participation phase. This phase

Figure 4.2 Primary, secondary, and minor trends.
Source: Bloomberg.

tends not only to be the longest lasting but also the one with the largest price movement. It's also the phase in which most technical traders start to take long positions.

Finally, market prices exceed reasonable valuations as greed drives "irrational exuberance." At this point the smart money that bought at significantly lower levels starts to exit the market as less sophisticated investors enter the market in search of easy money. As the market has made a strong move higher on the improved business conditions and buying by market participants to move starts to age, we begin to move into the excess phase. At this point, the market is hot again for all investors.

The last stage in the upward trend, the excess phase, is the one in which the smart money realizes profits and starts to scale back its positions, selling them off to those now entering the market. During this phase, a lot of attention should be placed on signs of weakness in the trend, such as strengthening downward moves. Also, if the upward moves start to show weakness, it could be another sign that the trend may be near the start of a primary downtrend.

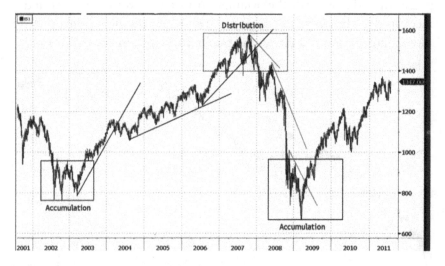

Figure 4.3   Accumulation and distribution.

The first phase in a bear market is known as the distribution phase, the period in which informed buyers sell (distribute) their positions. This is the opposite of the accumulation phase during a bull market in that the informed buyers are now selling into an overbought market instead of buying in an oversold market.

In this phase, overall sentiment continues to be optimistic, with expectations of higher market levels. It is also the phase in which there is continued buying by the last of the investors in the market.

From a technical standpoint, the distribution phase is represented by a topping of the market where the price movement starts to flatten as selling pressure increases. A new downward trend will be confirmed when the previous trend fails to make another consecutive higher high and low.

This phase is similar to the public participation phase found in a primary upward trend in that it lasts the longest and will represent the largest part of the move—in this case downward. During this phase it is clear that the business conditions in the market are getting worse and the sentiment is becoming more negative as time goes on. The market continues to discount the worsening conditions as selling increases and buying dries up.

The last phase of the primary downward market tends to be filled with market panic and can lead to very large sell-offs in a very short period of time. In the panic phase, the market is wrought up with negative sentiment, including weak outlooks on companies, the economy, and the overall market.

During this phase you will see many investors selling off their stakes in panic. Usually, these participants are the ones that just entered the market during the excess phase of the previous run-up in share price. It is at this point that shares get returned to the institutions at discount prices in a panicked fire sale. This is the smart money buying once more, if only by default. The cycle begins again.

4. The Averages Must Confirm Each Other

Dow theory states that in order for a trend to be considered valid, it must be confirmed by both the Dow Jones Industrial Average and the Dow Jones Transportation Average. The Industrial Average appreciating suggests goods and services are being purchased; if this is truly the case, then they should be transported around the economy too. Hence, the confirmation of both averages breaking to new highs is a strong sign of genuine strength in the economy. This means that both the industrial and transportation sectors of the market must be showing similar trends for the overall market trend to be considered reliable.

New highs in both the Industrial Average and the Dow Transports are often taken as a signal that a new bull market has begun, while new lows in both signal a bear market.

This non-confirmation of highly correlated prices gives a warning signal referred to as a "divergence." This concept is used when analyzing market prices with technical indicators such as MACD and RSI (more on them later).

5. Volume Must Confirm the Trend

Dow theory also emphasizes the importance of volume in confirming the validity of a trend. A trend is considered more reliable if it is accompanied by an increase in volume, as this indicates that more investors are participating in the market and supporting the trend.

According to Dow theory, the main signals for buying and selling are based on the price movements of the indices. Volume is also used as a secondary indicator to help confirm what the price movement is suggesting.

From this tenet it follows that volume should increase when the price moves in the direction of the trend and decrease when the price moves in the opposite direction of the trend. For example, in an uptrend, volume should increase when the price rises and fall when the price falls. The reason for this is that the uptrend shows strength when volume increases because traders are more willing to buy an asset in the belief that the upward momentum will continue.

Conversely, if volume runs counter to the trend, it is a sign of weakness in the existing trend. Again, Dow uses divergence signals as an early warning of trend weakness. Once a trend has been confirmed by volume, the majority of money in the market should be moving with the trend and not against it.

6. A Trend Is Assumed to Be in Effect Until It Gives Definite Signals That It Has Reversed

Dow theory states that a trend is considered to be in effect until it gives clear signals that it has reversed. This means that investors should not assume that a trend has reversed until there is clear evidence to support such a change.

The reason for identifying a trend is to determine the overall direction of the market so that trades can be made with the trends and not against them. As was illustrated in the third tenet, trends move from uptrend to downtrend, which makes it important to identify transitions between these two trend directions.

Traders wait for a clear picture of a trend reversal because the goal is not to confuse a true reversal in the primary trend with a secondary trend or brief correction.

Contrarian Theory

Contrarian theory in financial markets refers to the idea that investment decisions should go against the current trend or consensus of opinion among market participants. The approach is based on the belief that groupthink or herd behavior can lead to inefficient or overpriced markets, and that by going against the grain at the right time, investors can profit from market mispricings.

The basic idea is that when most market participants are optimistic about an asset, it may be overvalued, and when they are pessimistic, it

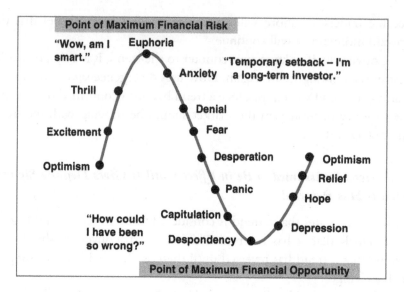

Figure 4.4 Points of maximum financial risk and maximum financial opportunity.

may be undervalued. Contrarian investors, therefore, try to identify and invest in assets that are out of favor or undervalued, with the expectation that the market will eventually correct itself and the value of these assets will increase.

In the following chapter we will explore some of the most popular techniques used for predicting market prices.

Chapter 5

Artificial Intelligence for Price Prediction

"AI is not going to take your job; a human using AI will."

—Unknown

rtificial intelligence has become extremely popular recently with the introduction of very impressive chatbots such as ChatGPT. These programs utilize an AI technique referred to as neural networks, designed to mirror human brain activity. The rapid improvement in their capabilities over the past few months has been astonishing. We are getting very close to a point in time where artificial intelligence may be able to convince humans that they are interacting with other humans and not a machine, in other words, when machines will pass the Turing test.

While these chatbots are very proficient at reading and writing, they are not very good at mathematics. In fact, there is evidence that over time they may be getting worse! A study from some Stanford researchers found that the performance of ChatGPT at accomplishing tasks in coding, mathematics, and reasoning deteriorated significantly from March 2023 to June 2023.

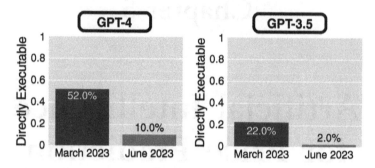

Figure 5.1   Performance of ChatGPT has deteriorated.
Source: Stanford.

Prediction vs. Classification

Artificial intelligence has many applications, but with respect to predicting financial markets, a clear distinction should be made between prediction and classification. Traditionally, classification in AI has been used for tasks such as visual recognition with great success, for example, deciding whether a picture contains a cat or a skin mole looks cancerous.

In financial markets it may be used to classify whether a market is in an uptrend or a downtrend. Studies have shown that this can be done with a high degree of success over the short-term for financial markets, proving the existence of trends and their identifiability.

Prediction, on the other hand, is more complicated, especially with respect to financial market data. The reason for this is the vast set of potential variables that can influence prices. Furthermore, stock market prices are a discounting mechanism, as traders process vast amounts of varying information, each with different preferences, emotions, and investment time horizons. Financial market prices are the result of this group negotiation.

Sharp price moves are seen when unexpected information and events are revealed. By nature, these factors are exogenous to the test sample data.

It is for this reason that long-term price prediction models are so difficult to create, even with the rapid innovation seen in the space.

Technical Analysis

The Chartered Market Technicians Association (CMTA) is a global body that promotes and accredits the use of technical analysis by financial professionals. They define technical analysis as follows:

> Technical Analysis is the study of data generated by the action of markets and by the behavior and psychology of market participants and observers. Such study is usually applied to estimating the probabilities for the future course of prices for a market, investment or speculation by interpreting the data in the context of precedent. (CMT Association)

This quote alludes to the belief that prices reflect the mood of market participants. As mass psychology of greed and fear are cyclical, it is possible to gain insight into future price movements from past price movements. John Murphy, the author of what is regarded as the preeminent text in the field, defines technical analysis as follows:

> Technical analysis is the study of market action, primarily through the use of charts, for the purpose of forecasting future price trends. The term "market action" includes the three principal sources of information available to the technician—price, volume, and open interest. (Open interest is used only in futures and options.) The term "price action," which is often used, seems too narrow because most technicians include volume and open interest as an integral part of their market analysis. With this distinction made, the terms "price action" and "market action" can be used interchangeably. There are three premises on which the technical approach is based:
>
> 1. Market action discounts everything.
> 2. Prices move in trends.
> 3. History repeats itself. (Murphy, 1999)

Murphy outlines the ideas first proposed by Charles Dow in a series of editorials written at the turn of the 20th century and published in the *Wall Street Journal*. He proposed that price is the true representation of all the actionable beliefs of market participants. He supports the idea that markets are cyclical, with price action often unfolding in a fractal and somewhat predictable manner. The most profitable of these is the trending nature of prices, which can provide an opportunity for market speculators to earn profits, an assertion supported by Kirkpatrick and Dahlquist (2006) as well as Pring (2002).

> Technical analysis is based on one major assumption: Freely traded, market prices, in general, travel in trends. (Kirkpatrick and Dahlquist 2006)

The challenge for market participants is to develop a quantitative trading strategy that shows profitable performance in past price action that persists during periods of future market price action that can be exploited for profit (Shiffman 2012).

Financial Market Prediction Models

A leading paper in the area of financial market prediction models by Choudry and Garg (2008) outlines the challenge of predicting stock market movements.

> Stock market prediction is regarded as a challenging task in financial time-series forecasting. This is primarily because of the uncertainties involved in the movement of the market. Many factors interact in the stock market including political events, general economic conditions, and traders' expectations. Therefore, predicting market price movements is quite difficult. (Choudry and Garg 2008)

Choudry and Garg highlight how stock market prices are the result of too many factors, both known and unknown, to accurately model with a high degree of success. However, the authors go on to state that there is a certain level of predictability due to the nonlinear movement of stock prices over time, more commonly referred to by market technicians as trends.

> Increasingly, according to academic investigations, movements in market prices are not random. Rather, they behave in a highly nonlinear, dynamic manner. Also, the ability to predict the direction and not the exact value of the future stock prices is the most important factor in making money using financial prediction. All the investor needs to know to make a buying or selling decision is the expected direction of the stock. Studies have also shown that predicting direction as compared to value can generate higher profits. (Choudry and Garg 2008)

Above, the authors explain that given the many factors that will remain exogenous with such models, it is very difficult to predict accurately what a price may be at a future date. However, identifying underlying trends may be achieved with a sufficient level of accuracy to make such pursuits profitable if done correctly.

> A trend is a directional movement of prices that remains in effect long enough to be identified and still be profitable. (Kirkpatrick and Dahlquist 2006)

ChatGPT and Price Prediction

Even the all-powerful ChatGPT admits that such future predictive proficiencies are beyond its capabilities. Our goal is to build trading algorithms and strategies that can run fully autonomously and generate consistent trading profits.

To do this, we create trading strategies that are suitable for the identified market conditions. It is then possible to change and test different parameters within these formulas to improve results. This process is known as parameter optimization. It is this big data optimization technique that offers the best profit potential when applying AI to predict

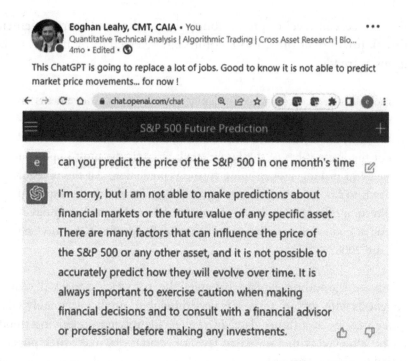

Figure 5.2 ChatGPT can't predict market price movements—for now.
Source: ChatGPT.

financial market prices. For this, we will employ an AI optimization technique called genetic algorithms that mirror the evolutionary process of nature to find optimal outcomes in a fraction of the time taken by the traditional brute-force optimization technique.

Chapter 6

Traditional
Trading Methods

"Plan the trade; trade the plan."

—Unknown

Having introduced the concepts of trends and discussed the
challenges of AI for market prediction, classification of conditions shows more potential.

There is a global accreditation body known as the CMT Association
that has been pursuing this goal for half a century, striving to turn mathematical techniques into tools for profitable market prediction. There are
hundreds of trading techniques and tools that all fall under the umbrella of
what is referred to as technical analysis.

There are many other useful analysis tools such as trendline analysis,
candlesticks, and pattern analysis that are useful for traders who are watching market price charts in real time and making trading decisions. We will
not be discussing them in this book.

In this chapter we will review the most popular methods that lend themselves to being used in automated systems as their rules are clear, nonsubjective, and easy to use for coding and parameter optimization.

They are:

- Moving Averages (MAs);
- Relative Strength Index (RSI);
- Moving Average Convergence Divergence (MACD); and
- Average True Range (ATR).

In the following chapters we will review sample strategies that have been built on the popular foundational technical studies discussed below, showcasing how these tools can be combined to build powerful market monitoring, trading, and prediction signals and strategies.

Moving Averages

Moving Averages are a common tool used in financial technical analysis to smooth out price data and help identify trends. A moving average is calculated by taking the average of a certain number of periods of a security's price. The resulting series of averages is then plotted on a chart along with the security's price.

There are several different types of moving averages, including simple, exponential, and weighted. Simple moving averages are calculated by taking the average of a set number of periods, such as the last 10, 20, or 50 days. Exponential moving averages give more weight to recent periods, which can make them more responsive to price changes. Weighted moving averages also give more weight to recent periods, but the weighting is typically more varied.

Moving averages are often used to identify trends by smoothing out short-term price fluctuations. For example, if a security's price is trending upward and its 50-day moving average is also trending upward, this may be seen as a bullish signal. On the other hand, if the security's price is trending downward and its 50-day moving average is also trending downward, this may be seen as a bearish signal.

Moving averages can also be used to identify support and resistance levels. For example, if a security's price is consistently bouncing off its 50-day moving average, this moving average may be acting as a support level. Similarly, if a security's price is consistently being rejected by its 50-day moving average, this moving average may be acting as a resistance level.

RSI

The Relative Strength Index (RSI) is a popular technical indicator used in the analysis of financial markets. It was introduced by Welles Wilder in 1978 and is used to measure the strength of a security's price action. It can be incorporated into a trading strategy to help identify potential trend reversals and overbought/oversold conditions.

The RSI is calculated using the average gains and losses of a security over a given period of time. It is typically plotted on a scale from 0 to 100, with high values indicating the security is overbought and low values indicating it is oversold.

To calculate the RSI, the average gain is first determined by summing the gains over the specified period and dividing by the number of periods. The average loss is then calculated in a similar manner. The RSI is then calculated by dividing the average gain by the average loss and expressing the result as a ratio. This ratio is then converted into a number between 0 and 100 using the formula: $RSI = 100 - [100/(1 + ratio)]$.

The RSI can be used to identify potential trend reversals, as well as overbought and oversold conditions. When the RSI is above 70, the security is generally considered overbought, while an RSI below 30 indicates an oversold condition. However, it is important to note that the RSI can remain overbought or oversold for extended periods of time.

In addition to identifying overbought and oversold conditions, the RSI can also be used to identify divergences. For example, a bullish divergence occurs when the price makes a lower low but the RSI indicator does not. This non-confirmation of momentum is a potential early sign that the current trend is losing strength and a reversal may be imminent.

MACD

The MACD (Moving Average Convergence Divergence) indicator is a popular technical analysis tool that is used to detect trend changes in the price of a security. It is calculated by taking the difference between a 26-day exponential moving average (EMA) and a 12-day EMA of a security's price. The MACD line is then plotted on a chart along with a signal line, which is a 9-day EMA of the MACD line.

One way to interpret the MACD is to look for a crossover of the MACD line and the signal line. When the MACD line crosses above the signal line, it is a bullish signal and indicates that the security's price may be starting to trend upward. Conversely, when the MACD line crosses below the signal line, it is a bearish signal and indicates that the security's price may be starting to trend downward.

Another way to interpret the MACD is to look for divergence between the MACD line and the security's price. If the MACD line is making new highs while the security's price is making new lows, it could be a bearish divergence and a warning that the security's uptrend may be coming to an end. Conversely, if the MACD line is making new lows while the security's price is making new highs, it could be a bullish divergence and a sign that the security's downtrend may be ending.

The MACD can also be used to identify overbought and oversold conditions in the market. When the MACD line is above zero and rising, it could be a sign that the security is overbought and may be due for a correction. On the other hand, when the MACD line is below zero and falling, it could be a sign that the security is oversold and may be due for a rebound.

ATR

The Average True Range (ATR) is a popular technical indicator that measures the volatility of a financial asset over a specified period of time. Developed by J. Welles Wilder, Jr., the ATR is widely used by traders and investors to identify potential trend reversals and to determine the appropriate levels for placing stop-loss orders.

The ATR is calculated by taking the average of the True Range (TR) over a specified period of time. The True Range is calculated as the greatest of the following:

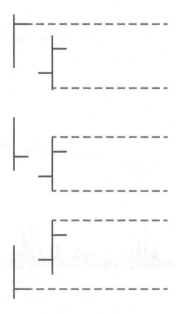

Figure 6.1 The Average True Range (ATR).

1. The difference between the high and low of the current period;
2. The absolute value of the difference between the current period's high and the previous period's close; and
3. The absolute value of the difference between the current period's low and the previous period's close.

The resulting ATR value represents the average range of price movement over the specified period of time, adjusted for any gaps in price movements.

Traders and investors use the ATR in a variety of ways. One common use is to set stop-loss orders. By placing a stop-loss order at a multiple of the ATR away from the entry point, traders can limit their potential losses while allowing for some degree of price movement.

Another use of the ATR is to identify potential trend reversals. When the ATR is rising, it can indicate that volatility is increasing and that a trend reversal may be imminent. Conversely, when the ATR is falling, it can indicate that volatility is decreasing and that the current trend may be continuing.

Overall, the Average True Range is a valuable technical indicator that can provide traders and investors with insights into potential price movements and volatility in financial markets.

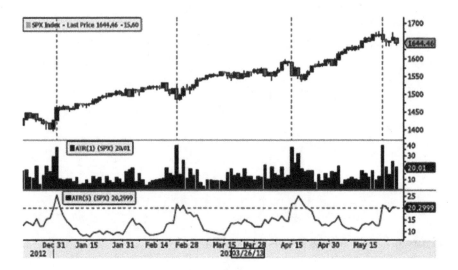

Figure 6.2   The S&P 500 with two different measures of ATR.

Figure 6.2 shows a chart of the S&P 500 index with two different measures of average true range. The ATR1, displayed as a histogram, compares the magnitude of the daily price ranges. Note how the largest daily ranges on the S&P 500 over the past six months have coincided closely with turning points.

The five-period ATR line is also useful at identifying turning points, especially near market lows. Toward the end of market corrections there tend to be large daily price ranges as extreme pessimism accompanies heavy selling. Once the market turns, short covering accentuates the reversal. The result is often an extreme reading on the ATR5, which captures the end of the capitulation and the sharp bullish reversal.

A key strength of ATR is that it adapts to the volatility of each individual security, so it can be used to create adaptive trailing stop losses. Creating a trailing stop using a flat percentage may not be suitable when applied to several securities with different market Betas. For example, a

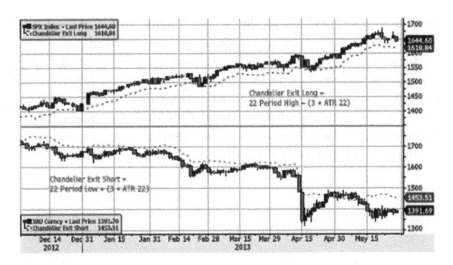

Figure 6.3 SPX index and chandelier exits.

trailing stop for long positions calculated using a recent high minus 10%
might be fine for a stock with a market Beta of one but too tight for
higher Beta stocks and too wide for lower Beta stocks.

One stop loss system that incorporates ATR is the chandelier stop.
This subtracts (adds) a multiple of the ATR from (to) a running high (low),
thus creating a trailing stop loss that can be used across securities with different Betas as the ATR adapts to the volatility level of each security.

Putting It All Together

By combining multiple technical analysis tools and analyzing multiple
time frames, traders and investors can create a more complete analysis
framework and potentially improve their returns. While each technical
analysis tool can provide valuable insights on its own, it is important to
combine multiple tools to create a more complete analysis framework.

For example, trendline analysis can help identify the direction of a
trend, while the RSI can provide insight into whether a market is overbought or oversold. Moving averages can help smooth out price data and
provide support and resistance levels, while the ATR can help identify

potential volatility and set stop-loss levels. Volume analysis can provide insights into market sentiment and potential price movements.

In addition to combining multiple technical analysis tools, it is also important to analyze multiple time frames. This is because different time frames can provide different insights into market trends and price movements. For example, analyzing price movements on a daily chart can provide insights into long-term trends, while analyzing price movements on an hourly chart can provide insights into short-term fluctuations.

Chapter 7

Advanced Trading Techniques

"Be greedy when others are fearful, fearful when others are greedy."
—*Warren Buffett*

ontrarian theory suggests that profits can be earned by trading against the crowd. Emotions drive markets to irrational extremes that present savvy traders and investors with lucrative investment opportunities. Warren Buffett likes to use fundamental measures to buy deeply discounted companies during times of crisis. Similarly, astute traders can identify multiyear price lows using the tools outlined in previous chapters.

In this section we highlight three advanced methods that can be used to monitor the trend of financial markets and identify profitable entry opportunities:

- Relative Strength;
- Market Breadth; and
- Seasonality.

Relative Strength Analysis

Relative strength analysis is a technique used to compare the performance of two assets or securities in order to determine which one is stronger or weaker. By creating a ratio of the prices over time, a chart is then used to compare the performance of the two assets.

There are several different ways to interpret the chart and make conclusions about the relative strength of the two assets. For example, if the chart shows that one asset has consistently outperformed the other over a period of time, it can be concluded that the first asset is relatively stronger than the second.

For instance, to compare the stock price of Apple to see if it has performed better than the S&P 500 index, of which it is a component, simply divide the price data of Apple by the S&P 500. If the line is rising over time, it means that Apple is generating better performance than its benchmark index. This outperformance is referred to as "Alpha." We will return to this concept later.

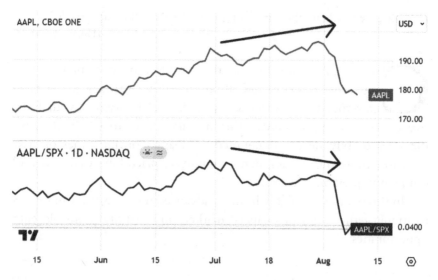

Figure 7.1 Price of Apple and Apple/SPX.

In the chart in Figure 7.1 we see the price of Apple in the top panel with the price of Apple divided by the S&P 500 index in the lower section. When the lower line is rising it means that the price of Apple is appreciating faster than the S&P 500 index, of which Apple is a constituent.

Notice how the trend of the lower ratio chart showed a lower high while the underlying price of Apple was still rising. This divergence signal was a good warning of future weakness in the price of Apple. In this instance it proved almost prophetic.

Bitcoin vs. the Total Cryptocurrency Market Cap

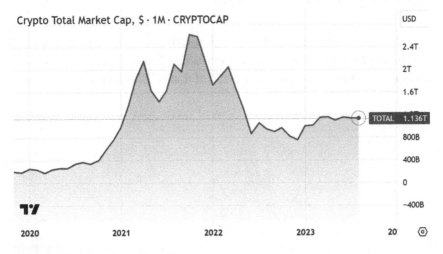

Figure 7.2 Crypto total market.

The market capitalization of the entire cryptocurrency market (Figure 7.2) represents the entire USD value of all the coins and tokens available for investment (as calculated by TradingView). This is the key headline figure that can be used to compare the crypto market to the market cap value of other asset classes.

The chart in Figure 7.3 shows the total market value of Bitcoin over time, while in Figure 7.4 we can see the comparison of the cryptocurrency market excluding Bitcoin versus the market cap of Bitcoin.

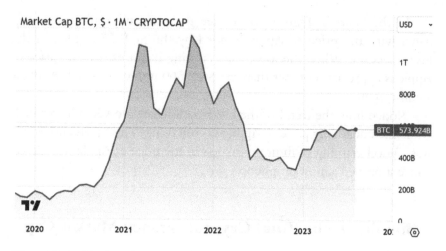

Figure 7.3   Total market value of Bitcoin.

In the chart in Figure 7.4 we break out the market cap of Bitcoin and compare it to the rest of the market excluding Bitcoin. We can see that in 2021 the market cap of altcoins exceeded that of Bitcoin for the first time.

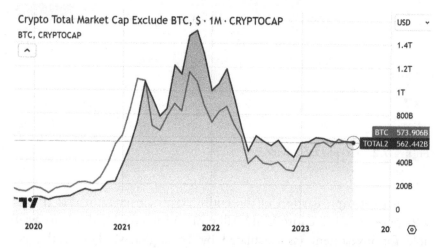

Figure 7.4   Market cap of Bitcoin vs. the rest of the market (excluding BTC).

Bitcoin is considered lower risk (Beta) than the smaller altcoins. As such, when investor risk tolerance increases, during bullish market price phases, investors rotate out of the safety of cash and Bitcoin into the higher Beta altcoins in search of faster profits.

This is a trend that is likely to continue in coming years as new technologies and coins follow in the footsteps of Bitcoin, increase in market value, and constitute a larger proportion of the total market.

If we break out the market cap of Bitcoin from the rest of the cryptocurrency market, we can see that it has now dipped to less than half the value of the total market cap. Many investors like to track the ratio of Bitcoin's market cap as compared to the total cryptocurrency market cap. This ratio is represented as a percentage and referred to as the Bitcoin dominance.

Bitcoin Dominance

The Bitcoin dominance percentage value really tells the evolution of the cryptocurrency story in a single chart. For many years Bitcoin made up over 90% of the market. It was the early success and adoption of Bitcoin that created the new space for other coins and projects such as Ethereum to grow into and follow in the steps of Bitcoin.

Bitcoin Price Performance versus Dominance over Time

Next, if we compare the chart of Bitcoin versus the chart of Bitcoin dominance, it is interesting to see that the drop in Bitcoin dominance to an all-time low of 37% coincided with the exact peak of the meteoric bull market of 2017. Here the exceptional price appreciation of Bitcoin really brought the cryptocurrency asset class to the zeitgeist. This allowed hundreds of other projects to be funded, which began to sow the seeds of the next wave of supporting cryptocurrencies.

The bear market that followed saw a record decline of approximately 90% for most cryptocurrency assets. Again, notice how the Bitcoin dominance shot up once more as both Bitcoin and the wider crypto market declined.

This suggests an inverse relationship between Bitcoin and Bitcoin dominance. Logically, this suggests that Bitcoin is viewed as a safer asset

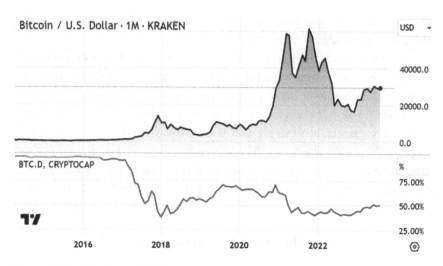

Figure 7.5   Bitcoin vs. USD.

than the altcoins. So when prices are falling, investors move out of the higher risk, smaller market cap altcoins back to the larger cap, less volatile (in crypto terms) asset: Bitcoin. Bear in mind, during sell-offs money is moving out of the whole asset class, meaning both Bitcoin and alts are falling, with the alts losing more value over the period.

Similarly, when the crypto market is rallying, money moves into both Bitcoin and alts. Yet we see alts outperform as investors favor the smaller cap, higher Alpha altcoins. In such an environment we see the Bitcoin dominance drop significantly.

This is similar to the relationship seen between gold and silver. During strong gold bull markets, silver tends to outperform as it is seen as higher Beta. Meaning it has a smaller market cap and more volatility, which results in higher risk, hence higher return, so long as the market continues to rise.

Past price action suggests the Bitcoin dominance falling tends to be bullish for the crypto market as a whole. This sounds counterintuitive, as one would expect that if Bitcoin is the best of all the cryptocurrencies, it should go up the fastest in good times. The reason is down to risk and return. When investors are more confident, they like to work their way up the risk-return frontier, chasing even more lucrative returns that can be offered by the higher risk altcoins.

As such, the Bitcoin dominance is a very useful tool for determining the strength of cryptocurrency market rallies.

Market Breadth—Metadata Analysis

Market breadth is a technique used to analyze the performance of the constituents within a market index, similar to how one might analyze the performance of individual players within a sports team in order to predict the outcome of a match. By looking at the overall performance of the team, rather than just the outcome of past matches, one can gain a better understanding of the team's potential future direction.

There are several ways to measure market breadth, but one common method is to use the number of stocks that are rising versus the number that are falling on a particular exchange. If the number of stocks rising is significantly larger than the number falling, it is considered to be a sign of a strong bullish trend. Conversely, if the number of stocks falling is significantly larger than the number rising, it is considered to be a sign of a strong bearish trend.

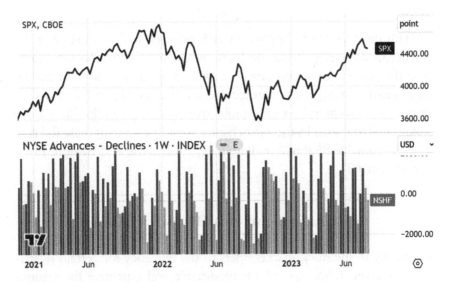

Figure 7.6   NYSE advance-decline line.

Other measures of market breadth include the advance-decline line (shown in Figure 7.6), which plots the difference between the number of advancing and declining stocks, and the advance-decline ratio, which is the number of advancing stocks divided by the number of declining stocks (Figure 7.7).

Market Breadth Measures
The following measures are available as numeric or percentage data fields:

ADVANCE & DECLINE DATA	PRICE VS. MOVING AVERAGES	MACD
» Advancers daily and weekly » Decliners daily and weekly » Unchanged daily and weekly » Net daily advancers—declines » Net weekly advancers—declines » Daily and weekly ARMS index » Advancing, declining, and unchanged volume	» Price greater than the 10-, 20-, 50-, 100-, 150-, 200-, and 250-day moving average » Price greater than the 10-, 30-, 50-, 100-week moving average	» MACDI greater than the baseline of zero » Signal line greater than the baseline of zero » MACD buy signal in last 10 days » MACD sell signal in last 10 days
HIGHS & LOWS	RELATIVE STRENGTH INDEX	BOLL BANDS
» New 4-, 8-, 12-, 24-, 52-week highs » New 4-, 8-, 12-, 24-, 52-week lows	» RSI 14-day greater than 70 (overbought) » RSI 14-day less than 30 (oversold) » RSI 14-day between 30 and 70 (neutral)	» Price above the upper Bollinger Band » Price below the lower Bollinger Band

Figure 7.7   Market breadth measures.
Source: Bloomberg.

This concept can be applied in various ways, such as looking at the number of advancing versus declining stocks on a given day, or examining the percentage of constituents making new highs or lows or trading above moving averages or other technical indicators. Figure 7.7 shows the wide range of technical breadth studies that are offered on the Bloomberg professional terminal. In the next chapter we adapt some of these fields to create a profitable S&P 500 trading strategy called the RSI Breadth Entry Trigger (rsiBET).

Seasonality and the Bitcoin Halving

Seasonality in the stock market refers to the tendency for certain securities or market indices to exhibit predictable and repetitive fluctuations in price and volume at certain times of the year. Technical analysts often look for patterns in historical data to identify and capitalize on these predictable seasonal market patterns.

There are several components that likely drive seasonality in market prices including economic indicators, holiday patterns, and weather conditions. For example, stocks in the retail sector may experience an uptick in price and volume around the holiday season, while energy stocks may see increased activity during the summer months when demand for electricity is higher.

The Bitcoin halving is a preprogrammed event that happens approximately every four years and reduces the rate at which new Bitcoins are created and added to the network. This is done by reducing the block reward that miners receive for adding a new block to the Bitcoin blockchain.

The block reward started at 50 Bitcoins per block and is halved every 210,000 blocks (about every four years). The first halving occurred in November 2012, the second in July 2016, and the third in May 2020. The next halving is expected to occur in 2024.

Multiple factors contribute to the observed seasonality and cycles in Bitcoin's price movements surrounding the halving event. First, the controlled supply resulting from the halving plays a crucial role. As the rate of new Bitcoin issuance decreases, the scarcity narrative intensifies, creating a sense of urgency among investors to acquire the limited supply of the cryptocurrency. This scarcity, combined with increasing demand or steady adoption, can drive prices upward during the post-halving period.

The purpose of the Bitcoin halving is to control the supply of new Bitcoins and maintain the scarcity of the cryptocurrency. The theory is that this will help to keep the value of the currency stable and prevent inflation.

There is a common belief among some in the Bitcoin community that the price of Bitcoin tends to increase in the months leading up to and following a halving event. This is based on the idea that the reduction in the supply of new Bitcoins, combined with steady or increasing demand, can lead to higher prices.

In the past, the price of Bitcoin has increased in the months following a halving event, but it has also decreased in some cases. For example, after the first halving in 2012, the price of Bitcoin rose from around $10 to over $1,000 within a few years. However, after the second halving in 2016, the

Figure 7.8 BTC/USD.
Source: Seeking Alpha.

price of Bitcoin initially declined before eventually reaching an all-time high of over $64,000 in 2021.

Bitcoin's price demonstrates seasonality and cycles, particularly with respect to the halving event. The pre-halving period experiences bullish sentiment and increased trading activity, while post-halving rallies often result in price surges.

Chapter 8

Automating Signals and Strategies

"If you torture data long enough, it will confess to anything."
—*Ronald Coase*

Making money in trading is not about perfection. It is about developing a strategy with a statistical edge and having the discipline to execute the plan without fail.

Trading is not about predicting the future like Nostradamus. Too many market strategists like to make unrealistic predictions that are not based on solid analysis. While such statements attract the attention of the media, they serve no practical use for traders and investors except to confirm their preexisting biases.

A casino will let you place large bets that are sometimes only 51-49 in favor of the house. It is possible for someone to walk in, place a single large winning bet, turn around, and exit with the winnings. This seems like a crazy business to operate. However, the casino knows that with enough bets over time, the odds will work in their favor. They trust their edge and their ability to realize it.

This is a good mindset to apply to building trading strategies. You want to test your ideas on past data to see how they perform. As most financial market disclaimers state, past data may not be an accurate indicator of future performance. It is, however, infinitely better than no data.

Quantitative Trading Strategies

The goal of quantitative trading strategies is to identify mathematical methods for analyzing past price data to generate trading signals that will be profitable in the future.

Quantitative trading consists of trading strategies based on quantitative analysis that rely on mathematical computations and number crunching to identify trading opportunities. Price and volume are two of the more common data inputs used in quantitative analysis as the main inputs to mathematical models.

The advantage of quantitative trading is that it allows for optimal use of backtested data and eliminates emotional decision-making during trading. The disadvantage of quantitative trading is that it has limited use. A quantitative trading strategy loses its effectiveness once market conditions change (Kuepper 2019).

Such systems allow for clear mathematical assessment and remove emotion by giving definitive trading signals based on mathematical techniques. However, they may be rigid and unable to adapt to changes in future market conditions.

Many quantitative analysts simply run large mathematical models to determine optimal strategies based on past data. They determine the perfect strategy for the test data, but often this strategy does not work well in the future data outside of the test dataset, referred to as the out-sample.

A more logical approach is to analyze the characteristics of the market that you want to trade and build a strategy around its characteristics. For example, if you are developing a strategy for a market that has been in a five-year uptrend, then a long-only trend-following system is probably going to work well in testing. However, if the trend suddenly changes, the strategy is unlikely to perform with success.

Such regime changes have been the death of many trading strategies as they fail to identify the new trend until it is too late and large losses have been incurred. Market classification is important. First define the characteristics of the instrument to be traded and the prevailing regime.

Traders must define a time horizon for testing, then determine whether the market is trending or range bound, the trend is up or down, the market is displaying high or low levels of volatility, and it is correlated closely with other instruments. Can you identify some unique characteristics that will give your chosen approach? Do you believe you have an edge that can lead to realized profits in the future?

When developing market strategies, it is important to first apply logic and then to test the data to select the right tools to profit from the identified conditions. Like a doctor analyzing a patient, if you only have a thermometer, you better hope the patient has a fever. However, with just one approach it is hard to determine what is the cause and how to approach the issue. An experienced doctor, just like an experienced trader, will test several vital signs, identify multiple potential issues, and then devise a remedy for success.

In this chapter we will analyze some examples of strategies that have been effective in certain market conditions. The skill is knowing when and where to apply them and how to identify when they are no longer working.

The Triple Exponential Moving Average (TEMA) System

This system has been used as it gives clear signals with fewer whipsaws than many traditional trend indicator systems such as Moving Average Convergence Divergence (MACD) and moving average crossover signals.

The bars are painted blue and red when the three averages line up to the upside and downside, respectively. However, it will leave the bars black when this condition is not met. This creates three signals; positive, negative, and neutral.

The bars in the chart are painted using the 4-9-18 triple exponential moving average (TEMA) system. This system generates positive trend signals (blue bars) when the EMA4 > EMA9 > EMA18; similarly, it gives a negative trend signal (red bars) when the EMA4 < EMA9 < EMA18. See Figure 8.1.

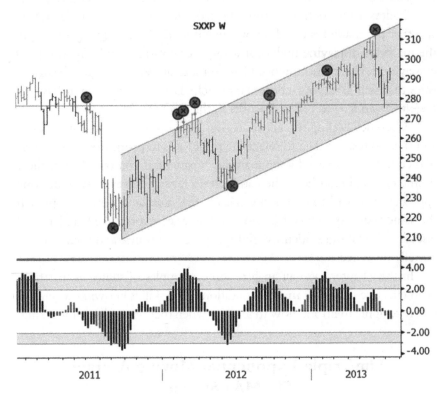

Figure 8.1   The TEMA system.

By design the TEMA system gives fewer signals as it requires all three averages to align from shortest to longest to generate a signal. This is in contrast to MACD and moving average crossover signals, which are binary, meaning they require less of a movement in the underlying to generate a signal, resulting in more false signals, especially in ranging markets.

A limitation experienced when using MACD and moving average trend systems is that by design they will be too slow to exit. As these are trend systems, their goal is to capture as much profit during sharp trend moves but not incur too many trades that lead to drawdown during sideways consolidations.

The steeper the trend moves, the later the exit will be, as the shorter average moves sharply away from the longer during the desired move and a contrary signal will not be generated until the averages converge and cross once more, resulting in a significant proportion of the gains being relinquished. See Figure 8.2.

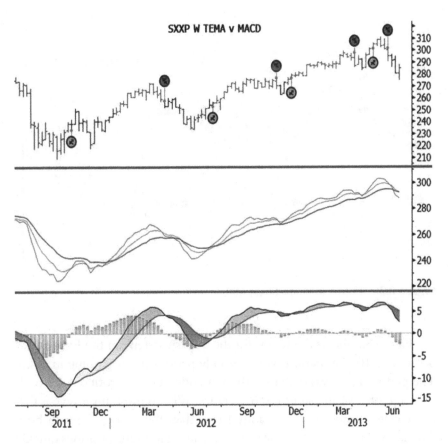

Figure 8.2   TEMA and MACD.

Notice how in the chart shown in Figure 8.2 MACD is giving both positive and negative crossover signals during the uptrend—six in total. From July 2012 the TEMA system gave positive and neutral signals but did not give a reversal signal until July 2013. Five MACD signals were generated before the TEMA system gave its second signal. Fewer trades mean less commission paid and less risk of slippage.

The system will enter long when EMA4 > EMA9 > EMA18 but will exit as soon as the EMA4 < EMA9. Similarly, it does not enter short until EMA4 < EMA9 < EMA18 and will then exit short once EMA4 > EMA9. By doing this the system will enter fewer trades and exit more quickly following successful trend moves.

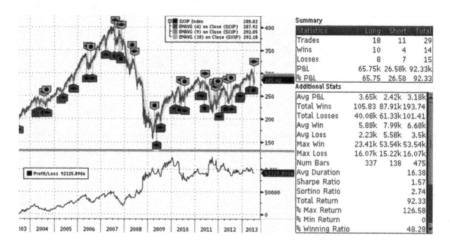

Figure 8.3   TEMA for Euro Stoxx 600.

Figure 8.3 shows the results for the TEMA system on the Euro Stoxx 600 over a 10-year period with a weekly periodicity, beginning in 2003. The performance was better on the long side but was profitable for both the long (65.7%) and short (26.6%) trades. What is most impressive is that the average winner is significantly larger than the average loser in both directions. This means that the system is cutting its losing positions quickly and letting winning positions run (but not too long). This is the key to a successful trend-following system.

Using the False Breakout Finder (FBF) Study to Find Potential Reversals

New highs and lows are of interest to a wide range of investors regardless of chosen asset class. Traders use these levels to trigger different actions depending on their time horizon. Many long-term investors look to buy breakouts to new highs as a momentum or trend-following strategy.

Short-term traders tend to scan the same 52-week high lists with the theory that a break to new high often exhausts buying volume and acts as a trigger for short-term profit taking. Both approaches are valid; the key differential is the investment horizons. To qualify as a breakout in technical analysis, the security in question should show signs of strength during the breakout. A sustainable breakout is often accompanied by a large one-day move through the potential resistance and high trading volume. Following such a breakout, the market moves and closes a set percentage from the breakout level or sees several successive closes above this level.

The False Breakout Finder (FBF) study hunts for the exact opposite situation: it aims to identify when a security has exhausted itself breaking to a new high and is now susceptible to a significant move in the opposite direction. See Figure 8.4.

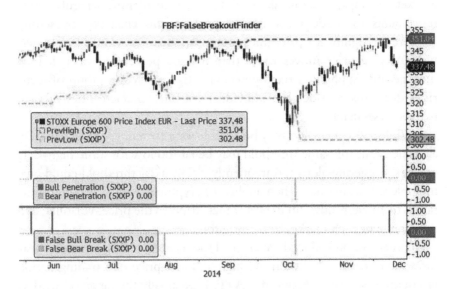

Figure 8.4 The False Breakout Finder.

The strategy codes two different types of signals; the first is referred to as a "Bull (Bear) Penetration." This occurs when the price action makes a new intraday high and closes the same day below the level of the previous high. The second is referred to as a "False Bull (Bear) Break." This occurs when price closes at a new high and then reverses to close below the level of the previous high within the following three sessions. These signals are highlighted in the chart in Figure 8.4, in the second and third panels, respectively.

Looking at the recent signals on the Euro Stoxx 600, the signals have done a good job at identifying recent market reversal points with both a Bull Penetration and False Bull Break occurring in the past few sessions.

This is not always the case. During sustained trending periods, many signals may be generated that do not lead to reversals. As such, this is a study that highlights potential trading setups and can be used as one tool in a larger analytical framework.

Monitoring the Market Sell-Off with Range Volatility Spike Alerts

Market participants across all asset classes try to identify irregular price movements for trade ideas. Many approach this challenge by setting an alert for significant price movement. An example would be an alert when any security moves more than a fixed percentage in a defined time period. Applying a fixed percentage figure across a group of securities does not consider the individual volatility characteristics of each market or security.

While a 2% price alert may be suitable for a currency, giving few daily alerts per year, this same threshold may be far too low for some high-Beta equities, triggering alerts too frequently, while a 2% threshold could give multiple signals per day when applied to cryptocurrencies! A better solution is to set alerts using an indicator that adapts to the price, volatility, and time frame of each market to be monitored.

Earlier we introduced Average True Range (ATR), which measures the difference between the high and low price of a trading period (accounting for gaps). A one-day ATR is essentially the range of the day, the difference between the high and low price. Daily price ranges tend to be modest during uptrend moves as the market climbs higher in an orderly fashion with limited volatility.

The RVS indicator compares a one-period ATR to an adjustable multiple of the 20-period ATR. This ATR methodology will adapt to the characteristics of any market, better identifying significant price movements while adjusting for the security specific volatility levels. See Figure 8.5.

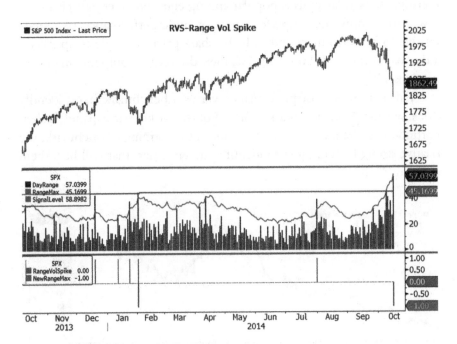

Figure 8.5 S&P 500 with the RVS study.

The chart in Figure 8.5 shows the S&P 500 with the RVS study. When the DayRange (ATR1) reading spikes above the SignalLevel (ATR20 × 2) an alert is triggered. The red RangeMax line displays the largest one-period ATR seen by the market in question over the past 250 periods.

A signal is also generated when a new range max is created. This figure highlights the maximum potential move the market may make and is a relevant number for traders placing stops to minimize the risk of slippage.

At market peaks and especially at market bottoms, the uncertainty of investors at such turning points manifests in wider daily trading ranges and higher values of ATR. Tracking such spikes in ATR can alert investors to potential market turning points.

Programming Signals to Identify 52-Week Relative Highs and Lows

Relative strength analysis is popular among equity market participants as a way to identify the outperformance or underperformance of a stock relative to its benchmark index. If the share price of Apple is up 2% on a day when the S&P 500 is up 1%, then the relative outperformance of Apple is 1%.

This comparison of performance versus a benchmark helps identify stock-specific Alpha less market Beta. Equity market participants, such as portfolio managers who are tasked with outperforming a benchmark, use relative strength techniques to identify outperformers that will help them generate Alpha.

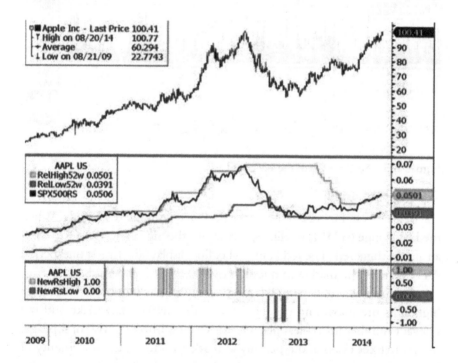

Figure 8.6   52-week relative highs and lows for Apple.

This study divides whatever security it is applied to by the S&P 500. Next, the 52-week moving maxima and minima are applied to the ratio with a one-period offset. If the current ratio high is above the 52-week relatively high as of last week, a signal is generated. A signal is also generated if a new 52-week relatively low is made.

We have already discussed the significance of new highs and lows above when discussing the False Breakout Finder (FBF). Searching for relative breaks to new highs is a good way to confirm breakouts in the price of the underlying. It can also be a good way to identify securities that are outperforming their benchmarks.

Backtesting Big Data—the RSI Breadth Entry Trigger (rsiBET)

The RSI Breadth Entry Trigger (rsiBET) is a market breadth study that endeavors to identify market sell-offs in global equity indices. Market breadth analysis involves aggregating characteristics of the components within an equity index. Using this big data analysis of the performance of the index constituents can provide a persistent edge over the traditional method of applying a technical strategy, such as the Relative Strength Index (RSI), to the overall index. The hypothesis is that analyzing the performance of the constituents within the index using big data can give more reliable signals than simply analyzing the performance of the index itself. The rsiBET study was designed to test this hypothesis.

Bloomberg produces a data field for the S&P 500 that records the percentage of stocks within an index that are registering an RSI study reading below 30 on a daily time frame. The rsiBET study triggers a signal when this percentage spikes two standard deviations from a 20-day average and then begins to mean-revert (by closing back inside the standard deviation band).

Figure 8.7 shows a 12-month daily chart of the S&P 500 index with rsiBET signals denoted in red. It is possible to simply look for extreme oversold readings to try and identify multiyear lows. However, by using the standard deviation to generate signals, the indicator successfully identifies quick sell-offs during bullish market phases. During quantitative testing this resulted in significantly better overall performance than simply applying the traditional RSI entry signals to the overall index.

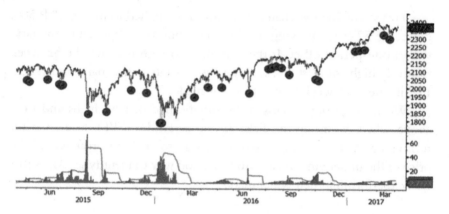

Figure 8.7 12-month daily chart of the S&P 500 with rsiBET signals.

The performance of the rsiBET study was tested on a 10-year time horizon using the Bloomberg Professional Terminal. The performance was impressive with 41 winning trades out of a total of 76, resulting in a winning ratio of 54%, with the average winner 1.55 times the size of the average loser.

Looking at the scatterplot in Figure 8.9 and the time series chart in Figure 8.10 we can see that the rsiBET long-only strategy outperformed buy and hold as well as traditional strategies that buy when the RSI value of the index crosses above the 20, 30, and 40 levels.

Converting Signals into Fully Automated Strategies

In this chapter we have introduced a number of market signals that identify potential profitable trading opportunities. However, to be a profitable strategy there are other considerations such as money management, risk management, and exit rules.

The process of converting trading signals into fully automated trading strategies involves several steps. Here is a general overview of the process.

Define your trading strategy: before you can automate your trading strategy, you need to have a clear understanding of what your strategy is. This includes defining the entry and exit rules, position sizing, and risk management parameters.

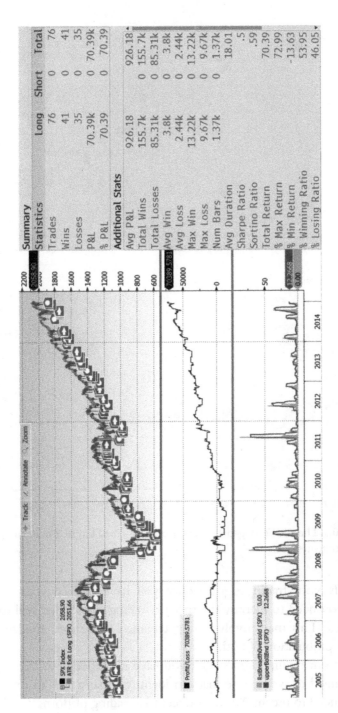

Figure 8.8 SPX index and ATR exits long.

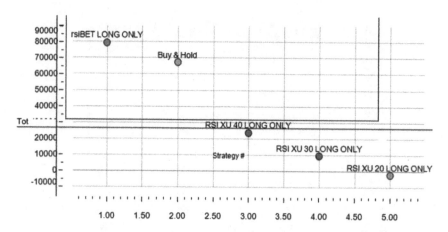

Figure 8.9   The rsiBET long-only strategy.

Figure 8.10   The rsiBEt long-only strategy outperformed buy and hold and several traditional strategies.

Identify your trading signals: once you have defined your trading strategy, you need to identify the specific trading signals that will trigger your trades. This may involve using technical indicators, fundamental data, or a combination of both.

Code your trading signals: after you have identified your trading signals, you need to write code that can identify these signals in real time. You may need to use an API to connect to a trading platform.

Test your trading signals: once you have coded your trading signals, you need to test them to ensure they are accurate and reliable. This may involve backtesting your strategy using historical data or using a demo trading account to test your signals in real time.

Build your automated trading system: after you have tested your signals and confirmed their accuracy, you need to build your automated trading system. This may involve integrating your signals with a trading platform or using a dedicated trading bot to execute your trades.

Monitor and refine your trading strategy: once your automated trading system is up and running, you need to monitor it closely to ensure it is performing as expected. You may need to make adjustments to your strategy over time as market conditions change or as you gain new insights into your trading signals.

Overall, converting trading signals into fully automated trading strategies can be a complex process that requires both technical and financial expertise. It is important to approach this process with a clear understanding of your trading goals, as well as the risks and potential benefits of automated trading.

In the next sections we will discuss advanced backtesting techniques in detail, giving an example of an advanced optimization technique that leverages a powerful artificial intelligence technique referred to as a distributed genetic algorithm.

Chapter 9

Backtesting and Optimization

"Only when you know the question will you know what the answer means."
　　—*Deep Thought, Hitchhiker's Guide to the Galaxy, by Douglas Adams*

We know the answer, but what is the question? When building a trading system, the goal is making money—this part is simple. The challenging part is asking the right questions and running the right tests to get there. Traders are constantly seeking the holy grail, hoping to find a single strategy that is going to give them winning signals across every asset class, market condition, and time period.

However, market conditions change, and there is no panacea, no single right answer. The skill is knowing the right questions. Identifying when a market regime is changing and it is time to use different methods to be profitable is the real "holy grail."

So you have been researching studies, have added them to charts, and feel you have found a methodology with some predictive power. Before committing real money to the strategy, it is prudent to do more analysis and stress-testing of the system before going live.

Quantitative Trading Strategies and Parameter Optimization

The goal of quantitative trading strategies is to identify mathematical methods for analyzing past price data to generate trading signals that will be profitable in the future.

Quantitative trading consists of trading strategies based on quantitative analysis, which rely on mathematical computations and number crunching to identify trading opportunities. Price and volume are two of the more common data inputs used in quantitative analysis as the main inputs to mathematical models.

The advantage of quantitative trading is that it allows for optimal use of backtested data and eliminates emotional decision-making during trading. The disadvantage of quantitative trading is that it has limited use. A quantitative trading strategy loses its effectiveness once market conditions change (Kuepper 2019).

Such systems allow for clear mathematical assessment and remove emotion by giving definitive trading signals based on mathematical techniques. However, they may be rigid and unable to adapt to changes in future market conditions. To create a profitable trading system, a key component is the selection of the parameters used within the strategy.

In the stock market, a technical trading rule is a popular tool for analysts and users to do their research and decide to buy or sell their shares. The key issue for the success of a trading rule is the selection of values for all parameters and their combinations. However, the range of parameters can vary in a large domain, so it is difficult for users to find the best parameter combination (Lin et al. 2004).

It is common for tests to be run on past market price data to find optimal parameter combinations that may be used to generate future buy and sell signals for the market in focus.

Through analyzing the stock market, we know there are some combinations of the parameters, which can produce a near-max profit and give some reasonable buy/sell suggestions. So, our objective in this paper is to find one of these near-max profit combinations efficiently (Lin et al. 2004).

The objective of backtesting and parameter optimization is to identify optimal or near-max profit parameter combinations using genetic algorithms. These parameters with the periodicity values selected for three moving average indicators are used in what Straßburg et al. (2012) refer to as technical trading rules (TTR).

The Technical Trading Strategy

The strategy to be tested is similar to the generalized moving average (GMA) rule used by Straßburg et al. (2012). However, instead of building a system that switches from long trades to short trades, a third, longer moving average (MA) will be used as a filter condition to first identify the trade direction, and then moving average crossovers will generate entry and exit signals.

Figure 9.1 shows an example from the Bloomberg Professional Terminal of the logic that will generate a long trade. For a long trade, the filter condition is that the current closing price is above MA3, a 200-period average in the example. If this condition is met, when MA1 crosses above MA2, an enter long trade is taken. Then when MA1 crosses below MA2 or the closing price falls back below MA3, an exit long trade will be taken. The opposite condition is then used to generate enter short and exit short trades (short trades are a bet on prices falling).

The logic outlined above can be summarized into four trading rules as follows:

Rule 1: Enter Long: enterLong = If((C>SMA3) && (MA1off < MA2off) && (MA1 > MA2),1,0);

Rule 2: Exit Long: exitLong = If((C<SMA3)|| ((MA1off > MA2off) && (MA1 < MA2)), 2,0);

Rule 3: Enter Short: enterShort = If((C<SMA3) && (MA1off > MA2off) && (MA1 < MA2),3,0);

Rule 4: Exit Short: exitShort = If((C>SMA3)|| ((MA1off < MA2off) && (MA1 > MA2)), 4,0);

Notice the offset is called "MAoff," which is the previous value for the respective moving average. This is how the crossing condition is programmed. So a bullish crossover occurs if MA1 crosses above MA2. To program this there are two steps: first that MA1off is below MA2off and then MA1 is above MA2. The value MA1 was below that of MA2 in the previous time period, but now MA1 is above MA2.

The Test Data

The multifactor trading strategy to be optimized will be applied to Bitcoin prices. The strategy will be based on the trading rules outlined above. Then combinations of input parameters will be tested to find an optimal combination with respect to the fitness function: percentage profit over time. For this study, daily closing price data for Bitcoin from the Bitstamp exchange from April 2013 to December 2018 will be used.

The data will be divided into three ranges:

1. Indicator creation period (04/2013–12/2014): this data is reserved for creating the moving averages before the test window signals are generated. It includes over 600 data points, which dictate the maximum periodicity that can be tested for the moving averages. The fact that Bitcoin trades 365 days a year means no

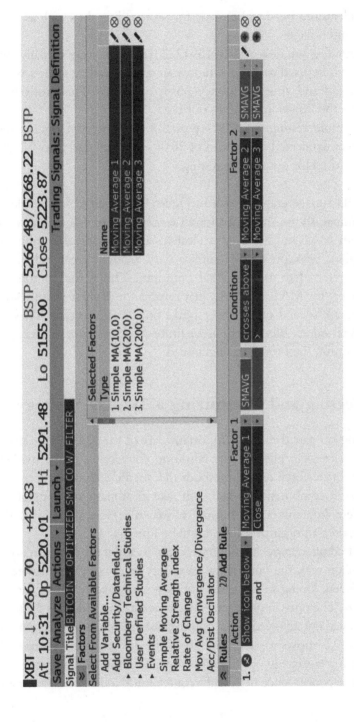

Figure 9.1 Bloomberg Professional Terminal Trading Signals: Signal Definition.

considerations need to be made for non-trading days such as week-ends and holidays.

2. Strategy test window (01/2015–12/2018): four years of daily price data will be used as a test window in which trading signals will be generated and an even money profit calculated. This profit figure will be the fitness function in our test.

3. Out-sample testing (01/2019–present): the potential test window has been truncated to the end of 2018 so that all data after 12/2018 can be used for out-sample testing.

The 3D surface graph shown in Figure 9.2, taken from the Bloomberg Terminal, shows the profit for all combinations of moving average (MA), both MA1 and MA2. It is clear to see the optimal combination as the highest peak on the 3D surface with a bright green value. This is what is referred to as the global optimum. This is the combination of parameters for MA1 and MA2 that returns the highest profit. Notice how there are several other lower peaks on the 3D surface. These are local optimal values. Bloomberg uses a brute-force method, so finding the global optimum (best result) is guaranteed.

Selecting and Optimizing a Trading Strategy

Backtesting on past data is an important part of the algorithmic trading system development process. The common convention in the market is to employ brute-force testing methods that inefficiently test every single mathematical combination, which can take exorbitant amounts of time to complete (remember the infinite monkeys!). However, this method does guarantee an optimal solution will be found.

For a trading strategy, it is often necessary to adjust the input parameters to better align with the underlying seasonality or cycle of the market data to be analyzed. Doing so can often improve performance during the out-sample tests. The out-sample is the exogenous data that followed the testing period but was not involved in the optimization calculation testing window.

Figure 9.3 shows a screenshot from the Bloomberg Terminal that shows the multi-strategy optimization page. This function allows users to compare the performance of 20 different technical indicator–based trading

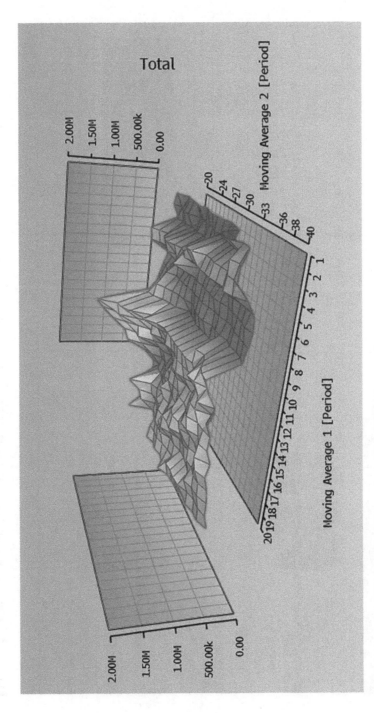

Figure 9.2 Bloomberg parameter optimization 3D surface graph.

XBTUSD Curncy   Add▾   Review   Actions▾   Backtesting & Optimization: Multi-Strategy

03/15/2017 - 03/15/2018   Today   Daily ▸

Table | Chart | Scatter Plot | Graphics Filter

Worksheet Title   BTST

«   ▸ Strategies | ☵ Columns | ⚙ Settings

Click here to see more details of the strategy.

The MACD was most profitable over the last year, with a simple buy and hold strategy coming fourth.

Strategy	Current Position	Age	Long	Short	Total	Total	%Total	Long	Short	Avg Duration	Profit Factor	Sharpe	Sortino Rat
Maximum		261	68	68	136	1.15B	1151.1	1814.55	336.56	261.00	10.22	51.26	95.2
Average	4.22M	27	12	12	24.52	180.04M	180.04	239.16	-59.13	28.74	1.63	8.41	14.6
Median	25.96M	12	7	8	15	96.48M	96.48	188.17	-87.04	18.20	1.21	3.35	5.06
Minimum	-174.38M	2	0	0	2	-129.27M	-129.27	0.00	-292.7	2.91	0.00	-0.70	-0.7
31) MACD	157.22M	4	5	5	10	1.15B	1151.1	1814.55	336.56	25.60	10.22	51.26	95.2
32) Fear & Greed	78.07M	5	8	8	16	653.45M	653.45	490.99	162.45	16.44	3.96	25.08	44.2
33) Weighted MA (WMAv	102.05M	6	7	8	15	603.02M	603.02	480.7	122.31	18.20	3.84	22.79	40.4
34) Buy & Hold	559.30M	261	1	0	1	559.30M	559.30	559.30	0.00	261.00	0.00	21.32	34.6
35) Simple MA (SMAvg)	86.41M	6	9	10	19	495.32M	495.32	535.94	-40.62	14.63	2.28	18.03	29.7
36) Variable MA (VMAv	73.79M	6	11	12	23	408.36M	408.3						
37) Ichimoku (GOC)	-109.88M	16	5	5	10	345.51M	345.5						
38) Triangular MA (TMA	36.13M	6	9	10	19	148.93M	148.9						
39) DMI	74.34M	46	8	8	16	146.93M	146.9						
40) Parabolic (PTPS)	34.54M	6	9	10	19	137.95M	137.9						
41) Accum/Distrib Osc	-20.79M	2	68	68	136	111.47M	111.47	188.17	-76.70	2.91	1.22	3.73	6.00
42) Rex Oscillator	37.41M	7	48	49	97	96.48M	96.48	204.50	-108.02	3.68	1.20	3.35	5.06
43) Exponential MA (EM	25.96M	6	9	10	19	78.81M	78.81	159.57	-80.76	14.53	1.51	2.89	4.51
44) MA Oscillator (MAO	33.32M	12	13	13	26	76.43M	76.43	163.47	-87.04	10.58	1.21	2.74	4.47
45) Rate of Change (RC	-17.89M	3	59	59	118	38.97M	38.97	179.06	-140.08	3.20	1.08	1.77	2.59

Zoom — ▬ + 100%

Figure 9.3   The multi-strategy optimization page in the Bloomberg Terminal.

strategies to identify which are working best on the chosen market over the selected time period and periodicity.

The most profitable Bitcoin trading strategy, using a daily periodicity, over the selected time range (15/03/17–15/03/18) was the MACD (Moving Average Convergence Divergence), which returned more than 1,151% for investors.

Bitcoin reached a then–record high of $18,674 in December 2017, before falling back sharply. The price spent several months in a range-bound market phase, making trading more challenging. The MACD strategy produced the best return over the test data period.

The MACD study uses the crossing of two lines to produce trading signals. The MACD1 line is the spread between two moving averages, usually set to 12 and 26 periods (which in this case are days). The signal line is the exponential average of the MACD1 line, which is generally nine periods by default.

By default, the MACD study uses 9, 12, and 26 as inputs. By changing these parameters, it may be possible to improve the performance of the strategy over the test period. The optimal MACD trading strategy would have picked up another 300 percentage points over the same period.

To identify potentially greater returns, we can test a number of input combinations to identify which set of parameters was most profitable over our test period. In Figure 9.5 we have created a series of backtests that will test every combination of MACD period 1 and MACD period 2 input parameters between the range of 5 to 40 and 10 to 60, respectively. This will run 1,836 tests, which we can then rank to determine which combination is most profitable.

Any of the first six iterations would have yielded the most profit, of 1,483%. This is 332% more profitable over the same time period than our initial strategy that used the default parameters, 12 and 26, which produced a return of 1,151%.

Figure 9.7 shows a three–dimensional representation of the entire dataset. Notice the stable plane that contains the most profitable combination. Sometimes when viewing the data, the optimal value is a sharp spike, suggesting it is more of an anomaly. By viewing the dataset in this way, we can clearly see the optimal result does not change much if the values are increased or decreased slightly. This is exactly what we want as it shows more stability in the result, increasing our confidence that this

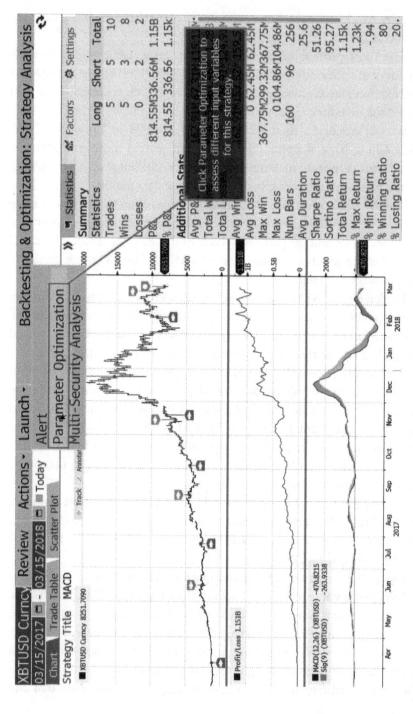

Figure 9.4 Parameter optimization in the Bloomberg Terminal.

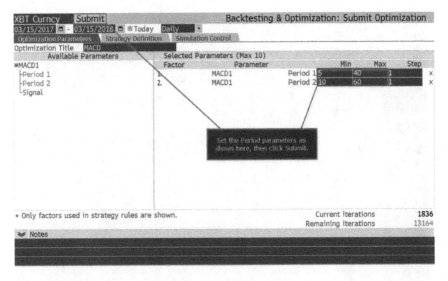

Figure 9.5   Backtesting in the Bloomberg Terminal.

optimal input combination will continue to provide improved returns going forward.

The chart in Figure 9.7 shows all iterations for the test sample. The X and Y axes are the range of input variables that create the MACD1 line. The vertical Z axis shows the performance of the strategy for each input combination. There is a plateau of returns surrounding the optimal input combination, suggesting that returns may persist.

While past performance is no indication of future gain, optimizing parameters on past data can significantly improve returns in the test dataset and may help traders to find the best input parameters for their chosen trading strategy. After optimizing for parameters, it is wise to test the new formula on out-of-sample test data that was not part of the optimized dataset to ascertain whether or not the new parameters provide better returns than the original set of values.

	Parameters		Current Position		Trades			Profit (Loss)				Avg	Profit	Sharpe	Sortino	Total	%
	MACD1 [Period 1]	MACD1 [Period 2]	P&L	Age	Long	Short	Total	Total	Total %	Long	Short	Duration	Factor		Ratio	Return	Re
Maximu			198.90M	5	15	15	30	1.48B	1482.7	1.03B	456.80	37.00	13.94	71.09	99.39	1482.78	158
Averag			33.98M	2	4	4	8.14	469.03M	469.03	389.18	179.86M	26.73	3.70	19.88	34.01	469.03	609
Median			53.25M	3	4	5	9	511.94M	511.94	438.30	84.70M	25.70	3.46	18.68	32.42	511.94	710
Minimu			-116.10M	0	0	0	0	-115.92M	-115.9	0.00	-115.9	0.00	0.00	-0.64	-0.65	-115.92	0.0
31)	10	29	198.90M	3	5	5	10	1.48B	1482.7	1.03B	456.80	25.60	12.85	71.09	0.00	1482.78	15
32)	11	26	198.90M	3	5	5	10	1.48B	1482.7	1.03B	456.80	25.60	12.85	71.09	0.00	1482.78	15
33)	12	24	198.90M	3	5	5	10	1.48B	1482.7	1.03B	456.80	25.60	12.85	71.09	0.00	1482.78	15
34)	13	22	198.90M	3	5	5	10	1.48B	1482.7	1.03B	456.80	25.60	12.85	71.09	0.00	1482.78	15
35)	14	20	198.90M	3	5	5	10	1.48B	1482.7	1.03B	456.80	25.60	12.85	71.09	0.00	1482.78	15
36)	15	19	198.90M	3	5	5	10	1.48B	1482.7	1.03B	456.80	25.60	12.85	71.09	0.00	1482.78	15
37)	13	23	190.68M	3	5	5	10	1.42B	1417.3	987.14	430.24	25.60	12.56	67.04	0.00	1417.38	15
38)	14	21	190.68M	3	5	5	10	1.42B	1417.3	987.14	430.24	25.60	12.56	67.04	0.00	1417.38	15
39)	15	20	190.68M	3	5	5	10			4430.24		25.60	12.56	67.04	0.00	1417.38	15
40)	16	18	190.68M	3						4430.24		25.60	12.56	67.04	0.00	1417.38	15
41)	16	19	190.68M	3	5	5	10			4430.24		25.60	12.56	67.04	0.00	1417.38	15
42)	17	18	190.68M	3						4430.24		25.60	12.56	67.04	0.00	1417.38	15
43)	11	28	177.48M	3	5	5	10	1.31B	1312.3	916.66	395.65	25.60	11.48	60.65	0.00	1312.31	13
44)	13	24	177.48M	3	5	5	10	1.31B	1312.3	916.66	395.65	25.60	11.48	60.65	0.00	1312.31	13
45)	10	30	177.24M	3	5	5	10	1.31B	1310.4	915.68	394.77	25.60	11.47	60.53	0.00	1310.45	13

Any of these six iterations would have generated the highest profit.

XBT Curncy   Resubmit   Review   Actions▾

03/15/2017 - 03/15/2018   ▪ Today   ▪ ...   Then click on 3D Surface for a more visual   Backtesting & Optimization : Results
representation of these statistics.

Table   3D Surface   Graphics Filter

Optimization Title MACD

☰ Columns   Statistics

Zoom — ▬ + 100%

Figure 9.6 Generating a 3D surface of the entire dataset in the Bloomberg Terminal.

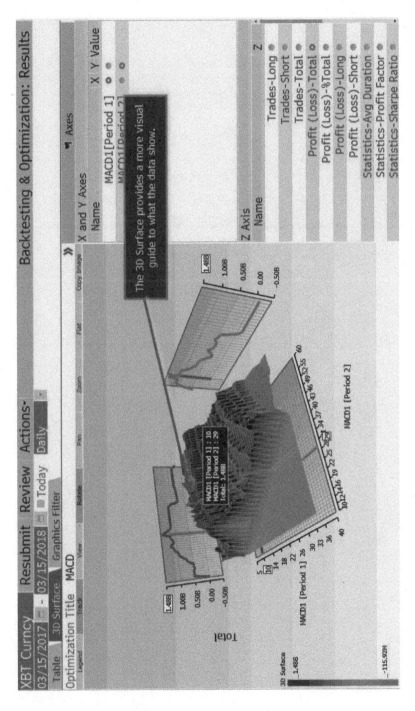

Figure 9.7 3D surface in the Bloomberg Terminal.

Chapter 10

The Evolution
of Artificial Intelligence

"It is not the strongest or the most intelligent who will survive but those who can best manage change."

—*Charles Darwin*

The rise of cloud computing combined with advances in microprocessors and AI have dramatically improved the speed, availability, and affordability of processing power. In the previous section we explored how to improve a trading program by optimizing the input parameters. This is a very powerful technique employed by professional traders to refine strategies and improve the risk-adjusted returns.

A complication arises when trying to optimize several different parameters at the same time with respect to each other. These jobs get very big very quickly. So big that a brute-force testing method becomes too slow to achieve results in a reasonable time frame. Let's examine how distributed, or parallel, genetic algorithms can be used to optimize the parameters selected for the technical trading rules found in quantitative trading strategies.

Infinite Monkey Theorem

People are notoriously bad at understanding large numbers. The infinite monkey theorem helps to portray the sheer scale of some of these factorial problems. Trying to solve these using a brute-force algorithm that tests every single possible outcome is often infeasible (at least within our lifetimes).

Figure 10.1 The infinite monkey theorem.
Source: Varut/Adobe Stock.

The infinite monkey theorem states that a monkey randomly hitting keys on a typewriter will eventually write the complete works of Shakespeare if given an infinite amount of time. However, the probability of this happening is so low that if the monkey started typing at the big bang, it is unlikely to have yet completed a single title. The excerpt below from *The Nature of Code* by Danielle Shiffman (2012) frames the magnitude of these problems eloquently:

> *Let's consider the phrase "to be or not to be that is the question" (we're simplifying it from the original "To be, or not to be: that is the question"). The phrase is 39 characters long. If George (the monkey) starts typing, the chance he'll get the first character right is 1 in 27 (twenty-six letters and one space bar). Since the probability he'll get the second character right is also 1 in 27, he has a 1 in 27*27 chance of landing the first two characters in the correct order.*
>
> *Therefore, the probability that George will type the full phrase is: (1/27) multiplied by itself 39 times, i.e. $(1/27)^{39}$ which equals a 1 in 66,555,937,033,867,822,607,895,549,241,096,482,953,017, 615,834,735,226,163 chance of getting it right!*
>
> *Even if George is a computer simulation and can type one million random phrases per second, for George to have a 99% probability of eventually getting it right, he would have to type for 9,719, 096,182,010,563,073,125,591,133,903,305,625,605,017 years. (Note that the age of the universe is estimated to be a mere 13,750,000,000 years.)*

Beyond Brute Force

The global financial sector is currently embracing a major technological upgrade as it moves toward cloud-hosted data solutions. Never has such computing power been so easily available. This creates ideal conditions for new and exciting datasets and artificial intelligence methods to be applied in ways never before possible.

Bloomberg is a leading data vendor in the financial data space (and former employer of the author—full disclosure). In the previous chapter we showed how it could achieve very impressive results with its backtesting engine.

Bloomberg offers a cloud-based product to clients that takes approximately 5–10 minutes to complete a multifactor optimization job that is capped at 15,000 iterations. This means that it can run the test a maximum of 15,000 times with different input parameters. Then one can compare all of the results to find the best settings for the strategy formula that achieve the desired outcome, such as maximum total return.

This method of testing every combination sequentially is referred to as an exhaustive brute-force method (which tests every possible combination). This method guarantees optimality but can be prohibitively slow; remember the monkeys writing Shakespeare above. Figure 10.2 shows an example of the output from a brute-force parameter optimization taken from the Bloomberg Terminal optimization function.

Genetic Algorithms for Parameter Optimization

A genetic algorithm is a search heuristic that is inspired by Charles Darwin's theory of natural evolution. This algorithm reflects the process of natural selection where the "fittest" individuals are selected for reproduction in order to produce offspring of the next generation. In this way, each new generation converges toward the optimal value referred to as the "fitness function."

Genetic algorithms (GAs) are a class of algorithms working on problems that cannot be solved in a deterministic and analytical manner. The main idea is to continuously generate varying solutions to a problem while combining, mutating, and evaluating them. Using this approach, it is possible to very quickly converge toward a desired behavior and to solve the original problem (Straßburg et al. 2012).

The Traveling Salesman Problem

The traveling salesman problem (TSP) is a classic example of the type of multifactor optimization problem that genetic algorithms are ideal for solving. Have you ever received a message from a delivery person saying

XBT BSTP Curncy	Resubmit	Review	Actions ▾					Backtesting & Optimization: Results

01/01/2017 🔲 - 04/10/2019 🔲 ☑ Today Daily ▾

Table | 3D Surface | Graphics Filter

Optimization Title   BITCOIN - OPTIMIZED SMA CO W/ FILTER   «   Statistics   »   ⚏ Columns

	Movi... Aver...	Movi... Aver...	Movi... Aver...	%Total	Long	Avg Dura..	Profi. Factor	Shar.. Ratio	Sorti. Ratio	Total Return	% Max Return	% Min Return	Wins in %	% Max DD	Max D... Length
Maximu				1772.0(	1.77M	62.60	17.09	5.95	9.89	1772.08	2425.01	0.00	83.33	62.43	115
Averag				686.80	686.80	41.92	6.88	3.34	5.20	686.80	1143.89	-1.58	60.73	38.62	58.44
Median				715.98	715.98	43.87	5.12	3.43	5.35	715.98	1181.10	-0.58	60.00	36.36	68
Minimu				0.00	0.00	0.00	0.00	0.00	0.00	0.00	0.00	-16.29	0.00	0.00	0
31)	1	20	190	410.20	410.20	18.86	4.12	2.69	4.18	410.20	612.20	-4.27	35.71	40.68	89
32)	1	20	191	410.20	410.20	18.86	4.12	2.69	4.18	410.20	612.20	-4.27	35.71	40.68	89
33)	1	20	192	410.20	410.20	18.86	4.12	2.69	4.18	410.20	612.20	-4.27	35.71	40.68	89
34)	1	20	193	410.20	410.20	18.86	4.12	2.69	4.18	410.20	612.20	-4.27	35.71	40.68	89
35)	1	20	194	410.20	410.20	18.86	4.12	2.69	4.18	410.20	612.20	-4.27	35.71	40.68	89
36)	1	20	195	410.20	410.20	18.86	4.12	2.69	4.18	410.20	612.20	-4.27	35.71	40.68	89
37)	1	20	196	410.20	410.20	18.86	4.12	2.69	4.18	410.20	612.20	-4.27	35.71	40.68	89
38)	1	20	197	410.20	410.20	18.86	4.12	2.69	4.18	410.20	612.20	-4.27	35.71	40.68	89
39)	1	20	198	410.20	410.20	18.86	4.12	2.69	4.18	410.20	612.20	-4.27	35.71	40.68	89
40)	1	20	199	410.20	410.20	18.86	4.12	2.69	4.18	410.20	612.20	-4.27	35.71	40.68	89
41)	1	20	200	410.20	410.20	18.86	4.12	2.69	4.18	410.20	612.20	-4.27	35.71	40.68	89
42)	1	20	201	410.20	410.20	18.86	4.12	2.69	4.18	410.20	612.20	-4.27	35.71	40.68	89
43)	1	20	202	410.20	410.20	18.86	4.12	2.69	4.18	410.20	612.20	-4.27	35.71	40.68	89
44)	1	20	203	410.20	410.20	18.86	4.12	2.69	4.18	410.20	612.20	-4.27	35.71	40.68	89

Figure 10.2 Bloomberg Professional Terminal backtesting and optimization results.

that they will be with you between 9 a.m. and 2 p.m.? This is a five-hour-wide window! Why can they not be more precise in their delivery time? Genetic algorithms are ideal at solving such problems.

The TSP involves a list of cities with the distances between each city also known. The driver needs to decide on the best (optimal) route that will see them visit every city via the most efficient (shortest distance traveled) route before returning home. In this scenario we are optimizing with respect to distance traveled: the shorter, the better.

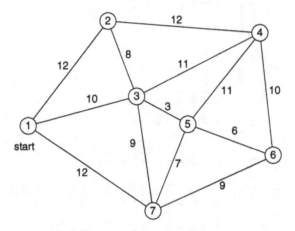

Figure 10.3   The traveling salesman problem.

This multifactor optimization problem is factorial in nature and, like the infinite monkeys, is prohibitively too large a job to solve using a brute-force search. The methodology that is used to solve this problem can be adapted to solve similar problems in other fields. We will use it to try and improve the profitability of a trading strategy by optimizing the input parameters.

Darwinian Natural Selection

Genetic algorithms are designed to mirror the process of evolution. Daniel Shiffman, who introduced us to the thespian monkeys, explains how the principles of Darwinian evolution underlie the logic that is used by genetic algorithms:

Before we begin, let's walk through the three core principles of Darwinian evolution that will be required as we implement our simulation. In order for natural selection to occur as it does in nature, all three of these elements must be present.

Heredity. There must be a process in place by which children receive the properties of their parents. If creatures live long enough to reproduce, then their traits are passed down to their children in the next generation of creatures.

Variation. There must be a variety of traits present in the population or a means with which to introduce variation. For example, let's say there is a population of beetles in which all the beetles are exactly the same: same color, same size, same wingspan, same everything. Without any variety in the population, the children will always be identical to the parents and to each other. New combinations of traits can never occur and nothing can evolve.

Selection. There must be a mechanism by which some members of a population have the opportunity to be parents and pass down their genetic information and some do not. This is typically referred to as "survival of the fittest." For example, let's say a population of gazelles is chased by lions every day. The faster gazelles are more likely to escape the lions and are therefore more likely to live longer and have a chance to reproduce and pass their genes down to their children (Shiffman 2012).

It is the representation of these three elements programmatically that generates the conditions for optimization that can be used to optimize the input parameters of trading systems.

Financial Applications of Genetic Algorithms

Genetic Algorithms can be used in financial markets in the following ways:

Problem-solving methods that mimic natural evolution processes;
Traders use them to predict stock prices;
Optimize data to identify the best values for security parameters;
Find the best-combined parameter values in a trading rule;
Can then be built into artificial neural network models to pick stocks;

Each trading rule's parameter is represented with a one-dimensional vector;
Each vector is like a chromosome;
Each parameter is like a gene , , ,
. . . Which is modified with natural selection.

Finding the best trading rules is a well-known problem in the field of technical analysis of stock markets. One option is to employ genetic algorithms, as they offer valuable characteristics towards retrieving a "good enough" solution in a timely manner (Chen et al. 2002).

To apply the genetic algorithm to a financial optimization problem, the data to be tested must be represented as genes in a chromosome.

10.1 Genetic Encoding

The data to be optimized is stored in a vector, which is referred to as a chromosome, while each factor to be optimized is referred to as a gene. The population is the entire set of chromosomes. A1 and A2 in Figure 10.4 represent parents that are creating children A5 and A6 by using a crossover method to exchange genes between the parents to create children.

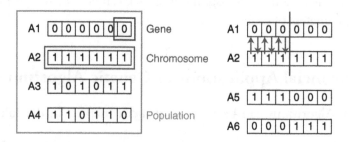

Figure 10.4   Components of a genetic algorithm.

Figure 10.4 shows an example of how these genes are then encoded into a vector. Different combinations of values within the gene will result in varying fitness function values.

	WTT	W	SMAC	W	MAD	
Chromosome	2	1	25	160	1	40	100

Figure 10.5   An example of a chromosome.

10.2 Types of Genetic Operations That Can Be Performed

Crossovers represent the reproduction and crossover seen in biology, whereby a child takes on certain characteristics of each of its parents.

Mutations represent biological mutation and are used to maintain genetic diversity from one generation of a population to the next by introducing random small changes.

Selections are the stage at which individual genomes are chosen from a population for later breeding (recombination or crossover).

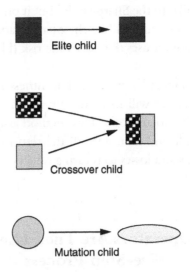

Figure 10.6   Crossovers and mutations.
Source: The creation of children, by Mathworks.

10.3 The Fitness Function

The term "survival of the fittest" offers a very accurate description of how genetic algorithms approach the task of optimization.

The term "fittest," however, can be a bit misleading. Generally, we think of it as meaning bigger, faster, or stronger. While this may be the case in some instances, natural selection operates on the principle that some traits are better adapted for the creature's environment and therefore produce a greater likelihood of surviving and reproducing (Shiffman 2012).

Examples of potential factors to optimize are outlined below. Each of these metrics could be potentially used for a fitness function:

Return on investment: how much money you earn, for each unit of money;
Drawdown: measures the maximum loss (in percentage) that the strategy has suffered over time;
Sharpe ratio: measures the reward-to-variability ratio of a trading strategy, allowing for comparison between strategies;
Sortino ratio: is similar to the Sharpe ratio, but it only penalizes the negative returns. It is calculated like the Sharpe ratio, but instead of the standard deviation, it uses the downside risk (Horta et al. 2010).

The above are standard measures. The fitness function used in the final code for this project will focus on return on investment (ROI) in the form of even value total profit. This method assigns an even amount of capital to each trade and then nets off the returns of all the individual trade percentage gains and losses to return a final percentage value, which is the fitness function.

These Three Operators Are Then Used as Part of a Five-Step Process

1. Initialize a random population, where each chromosome is n-length, with n being the number of parameters. That is, a random number of parameters are established with n elements each.
2. Select the chromosomes, or parameters, that increase desirable results (presumably net profit). The idea of the selection phase is to select the fittest individuals and let them pass their genes to the next

generation. Two pairs of individuals (parents) are selected based on their fitness scores. Individuals with high fitness have more chances to be selected for reproduction.

3. Apply mutation or crossover operators to the selected parents and generate offspring. The population has a fixed size. As new generations are formed, individuals with the least fitness die, providing space for new offspring.

4. Recombine the offspring and the current population to form a new population with the selection operator.

5. Repeat steps two to four. Over time, this process will result in increasingly favorable chromosomes (or parameters) for use in a trading rule. The process is then terminated when stopping criteria are met, which can include running time, fitness, number of generations, or other criteria.

The iterative process outlined above enables a genetic algorithm to drive convergence toward an optimal result. The iterative process is explained visually in the following figures. The algorithm begins by creating a random initial population, as shown in the figure on the right-hand side.

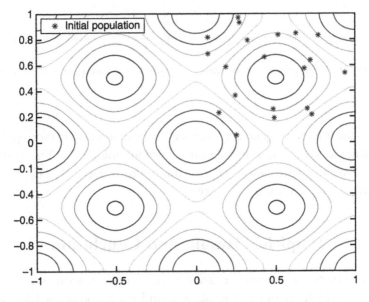

Figure 10.7   Initial population of values.

Figure 10.8 shows the populations at iterations 60, 80, 95, and 100.

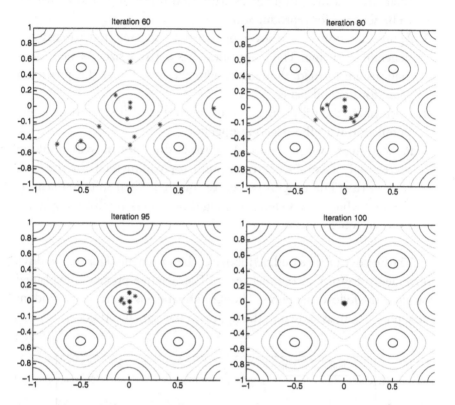

Figure 10.8 Visualization of genetic algorithm convergence from iteration 60 to 100.

As the number of generations increases, the individuals in the population get closer together and approach the minimum point [0 0]. This visualization shows an optimization where a minimum is the goal. The study for this paper looks to maximize profit.

Empirical Results and Conclusions

The barometer of success for any parameter optimization project is the speed at which an optimal result is found on a consistent basis when combining genetic algorithms and parallel programming to minimize the time taken to deliver an accurate result.

Preliminary tests showed optimal values being found using the genetic algorithm that is using a master/slave topology to distribute the workload across 12 processors. Several input variables for the creation of the genetic algorithm were hard-coded:

Genetic algorithm population size = 996;

Elite parents = 12;

GA maximum iterations = 45;

Number of processors = 12;

MA1 test parameter range = 1–100;

MA2 test parameter range = 1–100;

MA3 test parameter range = 1–100.

To run the code from milestone 3, "The Bitcoin Trading System Profit Fitness Function Solve Using Brute Force," a total of one million iterations of the fitness function were calculated. An optimal maximum even-money total profit of 668% was found using a moving average combination of 12-21-44 for MA1-MA2-MA3, respectively. This job took 1224.71 seconds to run.

The final test outlined in milestone 4, "The Bitcoin Trading System Profit Fitness Function Solved Using Genetic Algorithms and Message Passing Interface," was run 10 times. The best combinations, corresponding runtime and total percentage profit, are shown in Figure 10.9.

Test #	Best Iteration	Best Combination	% Performance	% of Optimal	Runtime (secs)	Speedup Multiple
1	12	13-21-44	662%	99.1%	1.52	806
2	1	10-22-44	658%	98.5%	0.13	9421
3	1	13-21-44	662%	99.1%	0.13	9421
4	19	12-21-44	668%	100.0%	2.45	500
5	4	11-22-44	654%	97.9%	0.52	2355
6	2	12-22-43	633%	94.8%	0.27	4536
7	28	10-22-44	658%	98.5%	3.58	342
8	5	12-21-49	613%	91.8%	0.64	1914
9	9	12-22-43	634%	94.9%	2.93	418
10	1	13-21-43	654%	97.9%	0.13	9421
Average	9.6	NA	650%	97.2%	1.23	3913

Figure 10.9   The Bitcoin trading system profit fitness function solved using genetic algorithms and message passing interface.

From the table in Figure 10.9, it is clear that the genetic algorithm with message passing interface is showing very promising early results. The genetic algorithm was finding its best value on average after less than 10 iterations. Notice that the combinations are all very close with only minor discrepancies between best combinations. The average performance return is 650% for the test period. The accuracy of 97.2% is calculated by dividing the realized return into the optimal return.

What is most impressive is the speedup: on average, the genetic algorithm is finding results 3,913 times faster than the brute-force search. Given that this job is being distributed on just 12 processors, such dramatic incredible speedup with a very healthy accuracy level is most impressive.

Unique Considerations of Cryptocurrency Trading

When developing a trading system, it is important to adapt the techniques to the market to be traded. Not all markets are created equal. Different asset classes, securities, and trading instruments will require consideration when adapting a strategy to a market.

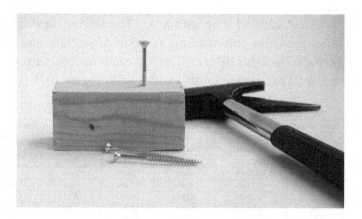

When trading Bitcoin, it is important to recognize some of the market characteristics that are unique to this market. Identifying these factors can help you develop an advantage and/or avoid potential risks.

Unique Considerations of cryptocurrency trading:

- Unregulated, subject to manipulation;
- Trading hours: 24/7/365;
- Not structurally sophisticated;
- Limited fundamental data available;
- Liquidity concerns: limited market depth;
- High-risk leverage ratios up to 100×;
- Automatic liquidations by exchanges;
- Trade execution orders freeze during high volatility.

All of the above factors contribute to high levels of volatility versus other asset classes and an overreliance on price data.

This price focus lends itself perfectly to bubble-like conditions where higher prices draw in more investors, who also expect higher prices ahead. This positive feedback loop where higher prices become the justification for higher prices is central to all historical price bubbles.

Putting It All Together—Bitcoin AlphaBot™

So far, we have gained an underlying understanding of why Bitcoin was created and how it works and have discussed methods for deriving a potential future valuation. Then we looked at some trading techniques for analyzing prices and identifying trends. Next, we discussed some common and advanced quant trading techniques that can be used as building blocks to create market strategies and fully automated trading signals.

Finally, we looked at parameter optimization techniques and reviewed how artificial intelligence can be applied to markets, in particular how distributed genetic algorithms can be used for large parameter optimization problems. All of the above lessons have been incorporated into the Bitcoin AlphaBot™ algorithmic trading system.

In the next chapter we will analyze a case study of a fully automated trend-following trading algorithm that has been optimized to avoid downside market volatility and capture profits from bullish trend moves higher.

Chapter 11

Case Study:
Bitcoin AlphaBot™

"Victorious warriors win first, then go to battle."

—*Sun Tsu*

Bitcoin AlphaBot™ is a fully automated trading system that combines human insight with AI-powered optimization methods to maximize risk-adjusted returns. The system was designed to profit from strong trend increases in Bitcoin prices while avoiding sharp market sell-offs.

Put simply, Bitcoin AlphaBot™ aims to "go to the party but stand close to the door!"

Bitcoin AlphaBot™ adds "Alpha" to your Bitcoin investments. Alpha refers to excess returns above the benchmark. The system is based on a proprietary trading algorithm built using artificial intelligence. It was optimized with a distributed genetic algorithm to maximize profit potential over time while mitigating the negative impact of risk factors.

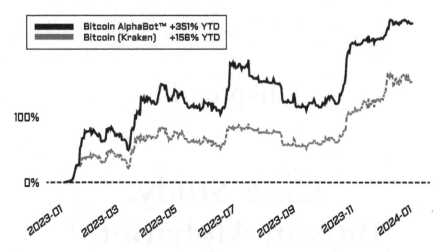

Figure 11.1 Bitcoin AlphaBot™ Cumulative Returns vs. Bitcoin.

The goal of the algorithm is to avoid high volatile turning points and quiet range-bound price periods. Investors are already holding Bitcoin, so they are exposed to the market "Beta" risk. Bitcoin AlphaBot™ strives to add low risk Alpha to existing Bitcoin holders.

Bitcoin AlphaBot™: Performance Analysis

To calculate the total investment return in US dollars we must combine the Bitcoin appreciation with the Bitcoin AlphaBot performance returns. That means since January 2023 your Bitcoin holdings grew by 76.5% while the dollar value of Bitcoin increased by 155.6%, providing a total dollar return of 351% (as of Dec 31, 2023).

Monthly Performance vs Benchmarks

Monthly Returns (%) vs Benchmarks

	JAN	FEB	MAR	APR	MAY	JUN	JUL	AUG	SEP	OCT	NOV	DEC	12M RTN
Eurekahedge Crypto HFI	25.6	1.6	7.4	1.1	(3.9)	4.1	(1.4)	(8.6)	1.6	16.4	15.9	3.1	76.47 USD
Bitcoin (source: Kraken)	40.0	(.0)	23.1	2.7	(6.9)	12.0	(4.1)	(11.3)	4.0	28.5	8.8	12.0	155.58 USD
Bitcoin AlphaBot™ - BTC	26.4	(3.0)	9.3	.8	(.0)	11.1	(3.8)	(3.8)	(2.7)	19.1	(1.9)	12.0	76.44 BTC

Figure 11.2 Performance of the Eurakehedge Crypto Hedge Fund Index and BTC.

The table in Figure 11.2 shows the performance of the Eurekahedge Crypto Hedge Fund Index and Bitcoin in dollar terms versus the performance of Bitcoin AlphaBot™ quoted in Bitcoin (BTC). This means that the Bitcoin AlphaBot™ performance is calculated exclusive of the appreciation of Bitcoin. All figures quoted are exclusive of fees, trading commissions, and slippage.

Bitcoin Alphabot™ Monthly Total BTC Returns

	JAN	FEB	MAR	APR	MAY	JUN	JUL	AUG	SEP	OCT	NOV	DEC
2015	-3.88	11.03	9.29	0.00	-5.88	6.30	-6.59	0.00	0.63	1.61	38.80	14.48
2016	-0.16	6.25	-0.90	3.10	10.08	30.66	-3.94	-0.89	-0.80	9.32	-2.88	23.12
2017	3.02	19.66	-2.78	8.39	30.05	-0.73	-7.65	56.44	2.44	30.29	39.38	32.86
2018	-1.89	13.47	-4.44	5.19	0.68	0.00	15.80	0.17	-3.61	-0.38	-0.89	5.99
2019	0.00	-3.93	-0.82	28.08	28.03	40.22	-1.34	6.22	-1.77	-3.13	0.00	-4.34
2020	3.23	-0.22	-3.79	5.15	14.54	-7.71	12.74	-7.94	-4.68	6.36	9.69	25.29
2021	12.85	13.96	8.35	0.38	-10.78	-3.77	5.55	-12.49	-11.07	23.92	-2.82	-4.24
2022	0.00	5.11	2.82	-2.14	0.00	-1.96	0.61	-9.83	-7.03	2.11	-1.19	-1.66
2023	26.35	-3.02	9.25	0.76	-0.01	11.09	-3.80	-3.83	-2.73	19.08	-1.86	11.98

Figure 11.3 Bitcoin Alphabot™ monthly total BTC returns.

The table in Figure 11.3 shows us the performance in BTC of Bitcoin AlphaBot for the entire sample period. This combines the out-sample performance testing data, which is derived from a real-time signal service that began in April 2020 (please contact us via www.quantmarketintelligence.com for access). Prior data is simulated using TradingView.

Notice that there are very few negative performance months. By being opportunistic as to when to enter the market, the system does a good job of avoiding sharp market sell-offs. Since 2015, the system has only participated in the market 14% of the time; this allows it to avoid many market sell-offs as well as range-bound price action that can destroy trend-following system performance—death by a thousand cuts.

When we combine the strong annual performance of Bitcoin AlphaBot with the market returns of Bitcoin, we can see clearly how

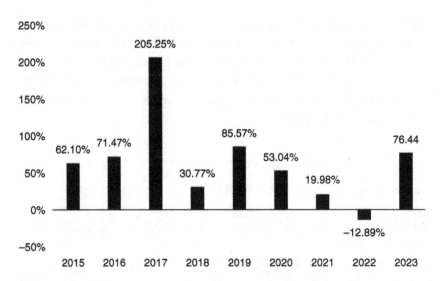

Figure 11.4 Performance of the Bitcoin Alphabot™ for 2015–2023.

past returns have been significantly enhanced: the "Alpha," which is the difference between the black line (Alpha plus Beta) versus the blue line (market Beta, aka Bitcoin).

Bitcoin AlphaBot was designed with the belief that Bitcoin is in a secular bull market (more on this in the next chapter) that will drive prices exponentially higher in the coming years.

Applying the Bitcoin AlphaBot™ proprietary trading algorithm to your Bitcoin holdings has enhanced total returns significantly since 2015, as shown in the chart in Figure 11.5. The reason for this is the system's ability to avoid the frequent sharp market sell-offs that plague Bitcoin investors.

Bitcoin AlphaBot™: Risk Management

A unique characteristic of Bitcoin AlphaBot is that it was not simply optimized for maximum total return. It was designed to avoid volatility and minimize losses.

As previously explained, genetic algorithms are an optimization technique that mirrors the natural process of evolution. They were applied to select optimal risk management parameters. Notice in Figure 11.7 how

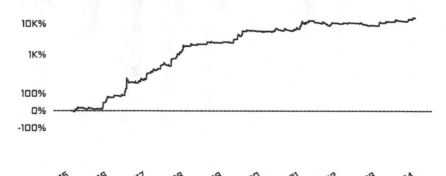

Figure 11.5 Bitcoin Alphabot™ cumulative returns vs. Bitcoin (Kraken) for 2015–2023.

the annual drawdown of Bitcoin AlphaBot™ (black) is much lower than that of Bitcoin (blue).

The performance of the algorithm was optimized using a distributed genetic algorithm to avoid sell-offs and minimize participation in sideways price ranges. The goal is to participate in strong upside trend moves

Bitcoin AlphaBotn™: Performance Analysis	
Number of Trades	456
Avg. Trades per Year	53.6
Time in Market	14.0%
Cumulative Return	13151.1%
CAGR%	77.7%
1Y	25.4%
3Y (ann.)	29.7%
5Y (ann.)	38.6%
10Y (ann.)	77.7%
All-time (ann.)	77.7%
Avg. Up Month	13.8%
Avg. Down Month	−3.8%
Win Days	39.4%
Win Month	55.8%
Win Quarter	67.7%
Win Year	88.9%

Figure 11.6   Bitcoin Alphabot™: performance analysis.

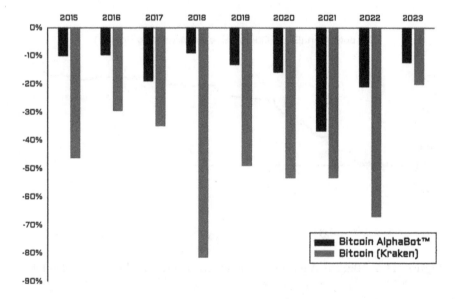

Figure 11.7   Bitcoin AlphaBot™ annual drawdown (%) vs. Bitcoin.
Source: Kraken.

while minimizing the impact of the devastating large drawdowns that are frequent in Bitcoin.

It addresses the uncertain price volatility by spending as little time in the market as possible. In fact the system trades about 50 times per year!

This is a sharp contrast to many high-frequency trading strategies that may trade 50 times per minute.

The improved risk management can be seen clearly in the monthly distribution of returns. There is a clear right translation to the data. Put simply, the distribution sees more outliers to the right-hand side, which represent large winning trades, while the left-hand side of the distribution sees much lower values, displaying clearly how the risk is being mitigated.

If we drill down even deeper into the data to view the bar chart in Figure 11.9 of the daily returns since 2015, it is clear to see that the upside moves are considerably larger in magnitude than the negative returns below the X axis.

Bitcoin AlphaBotn™: Risk Management	
Best Day	51.3%
Worst day	−10.8%
Best Month	56.4
Worst Month	−12.5
Best Year	498.8%
Worst Year	−13.2
Avg. Drawdown	−6.2
Avg. Drawdown Days	75
Longest DD Days	799
Avg. Up Month	13.8%
Avg. Down Month	−3.8
Win Days	39.4%
Win Month	55.8%
Win Quarter	67.7%
Win Year	88.9%

Figure 11.8   Bitcoin AlphaBot™: risk management.

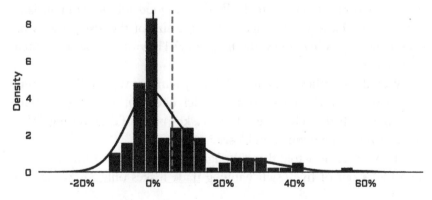

Figure 11.9   Distribution of monthly returns.

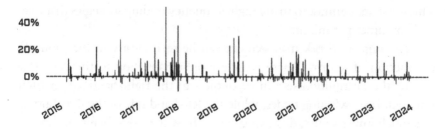

Figure 11.10 Daily returns.

Bitcoin AlphaBot™: Statistical Analysis	
CAGR%	77.7%
Sharpe	1.26
Sortino	4.49
Max Drawdown	−31.6%
Volatility (ann.)	36.2%
Expected Daily	0.2%
Expected Monthly	4.9%
Expected Yearly	72.1%
Kelly Criterion	22.4%
Risk of Ruin	0.0%
Daily Value-at-Risk	−3.6%
Payoff Ratio	3.57
Profit Factor	2.32
Outlier Win Ratio	29.98
Outlier Loss Ratio	2.01

Figure 11.11 Bitcoin AlphaBot™: statistical analysis.

Bitcoin AlphaBot™: Statistical Analysis

As seen above, Bitcoin AlphaBot™ does a good job at avoiding large losing trades. However, this shows that the size of the losing trades has been contained. What about the frequency? How often does the system make money?

Would you rather invest in a trading system that wins 80% of the time or 40% of the time? This seems like a trick question; obviously, winning more often is better. However, there is a key piece of data missing: What are the sizes of the winners and losers?

If you were now told that although the first system returns four winning trades out of five, each winning trade makes only $1, while each losing trades loses $100, while system two makes $100 for each winner and only loses $1 for each loss, which system would you like to invest in now?

Bitcoin AlphaBot™, by design is a trend-following system; as such, it is trying to capture large outsized returns, as shown in the distribution of returns graphics in Figure 11.8. The mission of such an approach is to run your winners as long as possible and cut losing trades quickly. This approach means that the system wins approximately 40% of the time; however, each winning trade is on average 3.6 times the size of each loser—this metric is referred to as the payoff ratio.

Sharpe vs. Sortino Ratio

Just as selecting the right strategic approach for the market conditions is vitally important, so too is what measure of success you choose to optimize for. A common measure of trading system performance favored by hedge funds is the Sharpe ratio. This is a questionable measure that has some distinct limitations for evaluating certain types of strategies.

Sharpe ratios reward strategies with high winning percentages but regular sized returns. For example, when trading Forex it is common to take short-term trades that "scalp" 20 or 30 pips out of the market. Such systems are ideal for measuring with a Sharpe ratio.

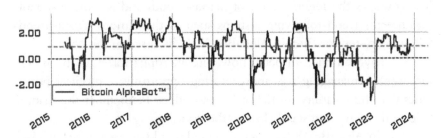

Figure 11.12   Rolling Sharpe.

Where the Sharpe ratio is less effective is when being applied to trend-following systems. The goal is to ride the trend wave for as long as possible. Should you do this successfully, you will have some very large winning trades that are multiples of the size of the average trading return.

Furthermore, with trend following, you will have a lower winning trade percentage and many small losing trades. These characteristics dramatically affect the Sharpe ratio measurement.

The critical issue is that the Sharpe ratio is penalizing good trend-following systems for doing what they are designed to do. The ratio does not distinguish between upside and downside volatility. If you are long the market, then an extended volatile price move in the desired direction of your analysis is exactly what you are looking for.

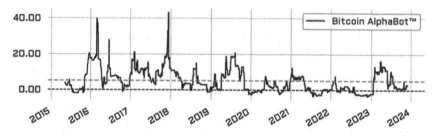

Figure 11.13   Rolling Sortino.

The solution is to use the Sortino ratio. It is similar to the Sharpe, but it does not penalize for upside volatility, meaning it is only concerned with drawdowns, the price moves that show as losses on a traders' P&L. It encourages the identification of market trends and is a more suitable measure for trend-following systems such as the famous Turtle trend-following system or Bitcoin AlphaBot™, as discussed in this chapter.

We have outlined in detail how Bitcoin AlphaBot™ has been very successful at managing risk and capturing opportunistic profit opportunities that the volatility profile of Bitcoin offers. Remember the mantra: "Go to the party, but stand close to the door."

Bitcoin AlphaBot™ has been designed to add excess returns in a bull market. In the next chapter we will discuss why the author believes Bitcoin has just begun a bull market that could last for several years and see Bitcoin surge to $100,000 dollars quickly. If this forecast proves correct, then the conditions are ideal for Bitcoin AlphaBot™ to successfully generate Alpha.

Chapter 12

Digital Asset Market Outlook—July 2023

"The market bottoms when the last seller has sold on bad news."

—Tom DeMark

I was fortunate to meet Tom DeMark and watch him speak on several occasions while we hosted him at Bloomberg. I remember someone once raised their hand and asked him, "So if all this stuff works, why are you not really rich?" to which he replied, "I am really rich, thanks for asking!"

DeMark's quote above refers to market turning points. He has proven adept at using his proprietary market timing methods to identify turning points with great success.

Often a new rally is attributed to a positive news story. However, the market price is a predictor of the future, not the present. It is an exhaustion of selling pressure at times of extreme negative sentiment that punctuates market bottoms.

It is interesting to note that two weeks after the FTX collapse in November 2022, the price of Bitcoin was trading back above June levels five months prior. Then the collapse of Silicon Valley Bank, the banker to many digital asset projects, barely affected cryptocurrency prices for more than a day or two.

These were two good examples of market prices ignoring bad news. This is usually the first sign of a new bull market. In the opinion of the author, the new bull market is already firmly underway and began in November 2022.

There are some significant bullish price catalysts that could drive the prices of Bitcoin and the entire digital assets investment space higher rapidly in the coming months.

Five reasons why $100,000 Bitcoin is coming faster than you think:

1. Sum-of-the-parts valuation too cheap;
2. Regulation is around the corner;
3. The halving is coming;
4. Synthetic short covering rally imminent;
5. Spot ETF to drive Bitcoin surge to $100k+.

1) Sum-of-the-parts Valuation too Cheap

"Markets can remain irrational longer than you can remain solvent."
—*John Maynard Keynes*

Sum-of-the-parts (SOTP) analysis is a method used to evaluate the cryptocurrency market cap by considering the individual components and their respective values. It is essential to assess the market accurately and ensure that the value of one's assets is not artificially inflated. Additionally, it is worth noting that the current crypto market is undervalued, a sentiment that even renowned deep-value investor Warren Buffett would likely concur with.

Currently, the total market cap of the cryptocurrency market stands at $1.13 trillion. Breaking it down further, Bitcoin holds a market cap of $567 billion, Ethereum stands at $223 billion, and Tether, the largest dollar stablecoin, which essentially represents fiat currencies, accounts for $83 billion.

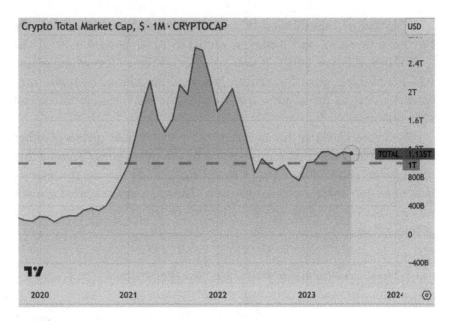

Figure 12.1 Crypto total market cap.
Source: TradingView.

Name		Price	1h %	24h %	7d %	Market Cap
Bitcoin BTC		$29,203.72	▼ 0.07%	▲ 0.07%	▼ 2.57%	$567.71B
Ethereum ETH		$1,854.08	▼ 0.02%	▼ 0.05%	▼ 2.81%	$223.12B
Tether USDt USDT		$0.9999	▲ 0.00%	▲ 0.02%	▼ 0.01%	$83.81B

Figure 12.2 Market cap of Bitcoin, Ethereum, and Tether.
Source: coinmarket.com; 7/26/23, 10:24 a.m., Irish time.

The market capitalization of the entire cryptocurrency universe less Bitcoin, Ethereum, and Tether is only $257 billion (USD) (= 1.13B − (567B + 223B + 83B)). If you consider all the cash reserves, goodwill, brand value, growth potential, human effort, Github commits, network activity, to name just a few metrics, the value should far exceed $257 billion.

A further kicker is that many altcoin projects hold tokens of other projects as part of their treasury reserves. As the saying goes, "A rising tide lifts all boats." Should the cryptocurrency market rally sharply, the reserves held in project tokens will also increase. This is an unrecognized growth catalyst that could really ignite a sharp recovery in the cryptocurrency altcoin space.

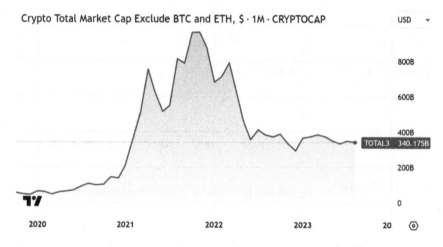

Figure 12.3   Crypto total market cap excluding BTC and ETH.

The chart in Figure 12.3 is the crypto total market cap excluding Bitcoin and Ethereum. This figure also includes stablecoins, which amount to about $120 billion at time of writing. This is the key chart to watch to analyze the performance of the altcoin market.

Despite the strong recovery in Bitcoin prices since November 2022, the altcoin market has been stagnant while sitting in the shadow of regulatory uncertainty. A more immediate driver of higher prices for the cryptocurrency market would be more regulatory clarity from the US regulatory authorities.

2) Regulation Is around the Corner

"Buy the rumor, sell the news."

—Unknown

The phrase "By the rumor, sell the news" has long been associated with the stock market, but it holds relevance in the cryptocurrency realm as well. As regulatory measures are anticipated, investors who wait for complete regulatory clarity before entering the market may miss out on significant gains.

The unregulated nature of the cryptocurrency market has allowed for practices that would be illegal in most traditional financial markets, such as "pump and dump" schemes and "stop-loss hunting." For example, the FTX exchange, designed to exploit regulatory weaknesses, engaged in cross-collateralization of positions to manipulate market prices and liquidate retail clients. The regulatory intervention aims to address such market manipulation tactics, protecting investors and promoting fair and transparent trading practices.

It is important to differentiate between Bitcoin, which can be classified as a pure cryptocurrency, versus other tokenized projects based on blockchain technology. These digital assets often involve initial coin offerings (ICOs) that attract investors with the expectation of price appreciation, an activity that is attracting close scrutiny from regulators such as the US Securities and Exchange Commission (SEC).

The SEC will likely focus on holding such projects accountable, particularly those involved in fraudulent activities or Ponzi schemes. For this reason, unless you have a clear understanding and insight into the altcoin market, it may be prudent to focus on Bitcoin as opposed to other tokens until more regulatory clarity is offered.

The digital asset market is likely to rally as traditional regulated institutions and professional investors buy in anticipation of favorable impending regulation. Therefore, being proactive and positioning oneself ahead of the regulatory announcements may prove a beneficial investment approach.

3) The Halving Is Coming

"It wasn't the trading that made the money, it was the sitting and waiting."
— *Jesse Livermore*

Bitcoin, as a decentralized cryptocurrency, exhibits distinct patterns of seasonality and cycles in its price movements, particularly with respect to the halving event.

The Bitcoin mining reward halving occurs approximately every four years and seems to have a significant impact on the cryptocurrency's supply and market dynamics. Some analysts suggest that the halving creates a supply-demand imbalance, where the reduced rate of new Bitcoin issuance, coupled with growing demand, drives prices higher over the course of several years.

The pre-halving seasonality is fueled by speculation surrounding the potential impact of the halving on Bitcoin's supply dynamics and long-term price prospects. Historical data shows that as the halving approaches,

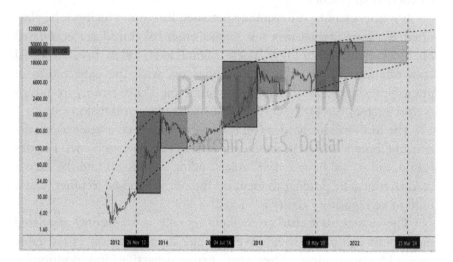

Figure 12.4 Bitcoin/USD.
Source: Seeking Alpha.

market sentiment becomes increasingly bullish, resulting in heightened trading activity and increased price volatility.

The chart in Figure 12.4 marks each halving event since the inception of Bitcoin. The seasonal nature of the price action has been depicted with different trading phases. First a rapid post-halving rally, followed by a sizeable and lengthy sell-off, before a pre-halving ramp-up. At present we have begun the steady pre-halving rally.

One of the most prominent patterns observed in Bitcoin's price movements is the occurrence of post-halving rallies. Following each halving event, Bitcoin experiences a surge in price, often leading to new all-time highs.

These post-halving rallies are characterized by heightened investor enthusiasm, increased media coverage, and an influx of new market participants. Notable examples include the post-halving rallies following the 2012, 2016, and 2020 events, which propelled Bitcoin's price to successive all-time price highs.

With the next halving expected in April 2024, it is likely that the pre-halving seasonal rally has already begun. Will this event coincide with a surge to new all-time Bitcoin price highs once again?

4) Synthetic Short Covering Rally Imminent

"Only when the tide goes out do you learn who has been swimming naked."

—Warren Buffett

Cryptocurrency markets lack the centralized authority and comprehensive regulations that govern traditional financial systems. This absence of oversight exposes investors to potential vulnerabilities.

The 2008 global stock market crash led to the US regulators enacting a temporary ban on the short selling of bank stocks, as a protective measure, to stabilize the financial system. In contrast, the unregulated nature of cryptocurrency markets lacks similar safeguards, leaving digital assets exposed.

As traditional regulated institutions enter the market, they will offer a range of products based on spot Bitcoin, further contributing to market maturity and investor confidence.

Synthetic products, such as Bitcoin and Ethereum futures and perpetual swaps, have gained prominence in the cryptocurrency market, but their presence poses risks without sufficient regulatory guidance and oversight.

It is also worth noting that they are merely contracts, so trading them does not involve the buying and selling of actual Bitcoin on the block-chain. As such, much of the market speculation of Bitcoin prices does not appear as transactions on the Bitcoin ledger; rather, it is side bets being settled off-chain.

The unwinding of synthetic products in the digital asset market, due to increased regulatory scrutiny, could have significant consequences. Reduced availability of synthetic products and heightened demand for spot Bitcoin held offline could lead to rapid price increases. This transition from synthetically created holdings to actual Bitcoin, which can be privately held offline in cold storage, is expected to bring more stability and credibility to the market.

This could cause a "squeeze" higher in prices as investor demand for Bitcoin significantly outweighs the actual available market supply. Think of the epic Game Stop and BMW short squeezes that saw eye-watering price moves in very short time frames. The structure of the Bitcoin market is ripe for a similar price surge as institutional investors flood into the spot Bitcoin market. The pending regulatory approval of a spot Bitcoin exchange-traded fund (ETF) will be a catalyst for a significant short-covering rally.

5) Spot ETF to Drive Bitcoin Price to 100k+

"Bitcoin should be equal to the total value of all the wealth in the world."
—*Hal Finney*

The lofty price prediction made by Bitcoin's creator, Satoshi Nakamoto, in conversations with Hal Finney, amounted to a potential $10 million per Bitcoin valuation back in 2008. Given the Federal Reserve balance sheet has increased tenfold since 2008 (see chart in Figure 12.5), this analysis would suggest an eventual price target of over $100 million per Bitcoin. An ambitious long-term target!

However, investors and traders are concerned with the current price trends over the next 18–24 month investment horizon. What will the

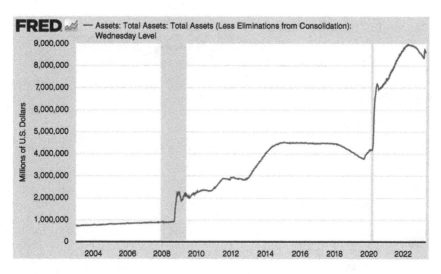

Figure 12.5 FRED total assets.

trend direction be and what potential upside and downside targets might be realized?

The impending approval of a Bitcoin ETF will drive trillions of dollars into Bitcoin. The average ETF holding for Blackrock has over $5 trillion in assets, which is 10 times the current market cap of Bitcoin in circulation and would give us a price target in the $250k–300k range. This impending tsunami of institutional money will drive cryptocurrency prices significantly higher.

Given the extremely low valuations, imminent regulation, pending spot ETF approval, upcoming halving event, and market prices that refuse to fall lower on bad news, there are numerous catalysts that will trigger higher prices in Bitcoin. It is the author's belief that the $15,471 bitcoin price low reached on November 21, 2022, may never be broken again. A new bull market has already begun that could see prices rise quickly to new all-time highs.

A key signal that will serve as a canary in the coal mine for the strength of the Bitcoin rally is the Bitcoin dominance percentage. This ratio looks at the percentage of the total crypto market capitalization that is contributed by Bitcoin. At present it is just above 50%.

The chart in Figure 12.6 shows the price of Bitcoin on the top pane, followed by the Bitcoin dominance value in percent and the total crypto market capitalization excluding Bitcoin and Ethereum.

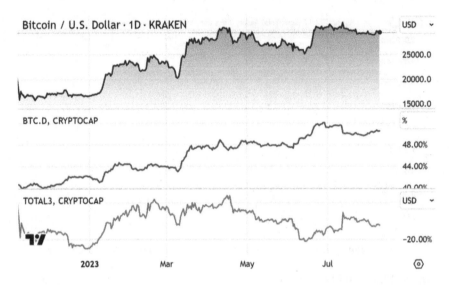

Figure 12.6   Bitcoin/USD.

It is clear to see that for the duration of the rally since November 2023, higher prices in Bitcoin have been accompanied by a rising Bitcoin dominance. Meanwhile, the rest of the cryptocurrency market has been trading sideways. This suggests that investors are still cautious.

To have confidence that the rally is ready to accelerate higher we need to see a breakout to new highs in the rest of the cryptocurrency market, exclusive of Bitcoin and Ethereum. In a bull market this would involve the entire cryptocurrency market rallying higher while the Bitcoin dominance is falling. It is worth watching the Bitcoin dominance value closely to navigate the impending bull market.

While Satoshi's $100 million per Bitcoin target may still be some time away from being realized, the $100,000 price level may be closer than you think!

References

Binance Academy. (n.d.). "What Is the Blockchain Trilemma?" https://academy.binance.com/en/articles/what-is-the-blockchain-trilemma.

Biswas, S. (2020). "Determining Bitcoin's Value with Science and Data." https://medium.com/coinmonks/determining-bitcoins-value-with-science-data-d514a7aee524.

Bitcoin Wiki. (n.d.). "Elliptic Curve Digital Signature Algorithm." https://en.bitcoin.it/wiki/Elliptic_Curve_Digital_Signature_Algorithm#:~:text=Elliptic%20Curve%20Digital%20Signature%20Algorithm%20or%20ECDSA%20is%20a%20cryptographic,order%20and%20hash%20function%20used.

Bitcoin.com. (n.d.). "A Deep Dive into Satoshi's 11 Year Old Bitcoin Genesis Block." https://news.bitcoin.com/a-deep-dive-into-satoshis-11-year-old-bitcoin-genesis-block.

Bitnodes. (n.d.). "Bitnodes." https://bitnodes.io/#google_vignette.

Bloomberg. (2017, November 30). "Goldman CEO: If Bitcoin Works, 'We'll Get to It.'" [Video]. https://www.bloomberg.com/news/videos/2017-11-30/goldman-ceo-if-bitcoin-works-we-ll-get-to-it-video.

Briscoe, B., A. Odlyzko, and B. Tilly. (July 2006). "Metcalfe's Law Is Wrong." IEEE Spectrum 2006(7):26–31.

Chartered Market Technicians (CMT) Association. (n.d.). "Definition of Technical Analysis." CMT Constitution. https://tanassociation.org/wp-content/uploads/2019/09/CMT-Association-Constitution-and-By-Laws-AMENDED-190311.pdf.

Choudhry, R., and K. Garg. (2008). "A Hybrid Machine Learning System for Stock Market Forecasting." *World Academy of Science, Engineering and Technology* 39, 315–318.

Coinbase. (n.d.). "Proof-of-Work vs Proof-of-Stake: What Is the Difference?" https://www.coindesk.com/learn/proof-of-work-vs-proof-of-stake-what-is-the-difference/.

Coindesk. (2020). "Previously Unpublished Emails of Satoshi Nakamoto Present a New Puzzle." https://www.coindesk.com/markets/2020/11/26/previously-unpublished-emails-of-satoshi-nakamoto-present-a-new-puzzle/.

Coindesk. (2022). "The Ethereum Merge Is Done: Did It Work?" https://www.coindesk.com/tech/2022/09/15/the-ethereum-merge-is-done-did-it-work/.

Coingeek. (n.d.). "The Mystery of the Genesis Block." https://coingeek.com/the-mystery-of-the-genesis-block/#:~:text=The%20Genesis%20block%20is%20shrouded,it%20to%20January%203%2C%202009.

Cointelegraph. (n.d.). "Bitcoin vs Ethereum: Key Differences Between BTC and ETH." https://cointelegraph.com/ethereum-for-beginners/bitcoin-vs-ethereum-key-differences-between-btc-and-eth.

Cointelegraph. (n.d.). "Proof-of-Stake vs Proof-of-Work: Differences Explained." https://cointelegraph.com/blockchain-for-beginners/proof-of-stake-vs-proof-of-work:-differences-explained.

Columbia University. (2022). "Cryptocurrency Energy." https://news.climate.columbia.edu/2022/05/04/cryptocurrency-energy/.

Crypto.com. (n.d.). "Blockchain Scalability." https://crypto.com/university/blockchain-scalability#:~:text=The%20Transaction%20Speed%20of%20Cryptocurrencies&text=While%20Visa%20can%20process%20up,capability%20to%20achieve%20mass%20adoption.

Crypto.com. (n.d.). "Consensus Mechanisms in Blockchain." https://crypto.com/university/consensus-mechanisms-in-blockchain?utm_source=lnkd&utm_medium=social&utm_campaign=sep10_consensuscharts_lnkd.

Del Vecchio, M. (2020). "Bitcoin's Stock-to-Flow Model Predicts a $288,000 Price Tag. Here's What That Means." https://www.forbes.com/advisor/investing/cryptocurrency/bitcoin-stock-to-flow-model/.

Deutsche Welle. (2021). "Why Does Bitcoin Need More Energy Than Whole Countries?" https://www.dw.com/en/why-does-bitcoin-need-more-energy-than-whole-countries/a-56573390.

Edwards, R.D., and J. Magee. (1948). *Technical Analysis of Stock Trends.* CRC Press.

Finimize. (n.d.). "Five Ways to Value Bitcoin." https://go.finimize.com/wp/guides/five-ways-to-value-bitcoin/.

Giustina, R. (2022). [Twitter post]. https://twitter.com/RaoulGMI/status/1502638102002782213/photo/1.

Grayscale Research. (2020). Valuing Bitcoin. Retrieved from https://www.lopp.net/pdf/theses/Grayscale-Valuing-Bitcoin.pdf.

Harvey, C.R., T. Abou Zeid, T. Draaisma, M. Luk, H. Neville, A. Rzym, and O. van Hemert. (2022). "An Investor's Guide to Crypto." https://coinmarketcap.com/.

https://seekingalpha.com/article/4481314-bitcoin-halving-cycle-resumes-backed-fundamental-catalysts.

https://theconversation.com/bitcoin-has-shot-up-50-since-the-new-year-but-heres-why-new-lows-are-probably-still-ahead-198682.

https://www.centralbank.ie/consumer-hub/explainers/what-are-cryptocurrencies-like-bitcoin.

https://www.coindesk.com/powered-by-consensus/crypto-regulation-new-laws-2023/.

https://www.forbes.com/sites/javierpaz/2022/08/26/more-than-half-of-all-bitcoin-trades-are-fake/.

Investopedia. (2004, April 21). "The Greatest Investors: Jesse Livermore." https://www.investopedia.com/articles/trading/04/042104.asp.

Investopedia. (2008). "Return of the Nakamoto White Paper: Bitcoin's 10th Birthday." https://www.investopedia.com/tech/return-nakamoto-white-paper-bitcoins-10th-birthday/.

Investopedia. (2021). "Automated Trading." https://www.investopedia.com/terms/a/automated-trading.asp.

Investopedia. (n.d.). "How Bitcoin Works." https://www.investopedia.com/news/how-bitcoin-works/.

Investopedia. (n.d.). "How Does Bitcoin Mining Work?" https://www.investopedia.com/tech/how-does-bitcoin-mining-work/.

Investopedia. (n.d.). "Relative Strength Index—RSI." Retrieved March 13, 2023. https://www.investopedia.com/terms/r/rsi.asp.

Investopedia. (n.d.). "Technical Analysis." Retrieved March 13, 2023. https://www.investopedia.com/terms/t/technicalanalysis.asp.

Jones, P.T. (2020). "Paul Tudor Jones BVI Letter: Macro Outlook Early May 2020." https://www.docdroid.net/2nTB6aY/may-2020-bvi-letter-macro-outlook-pdf.

Jones, P., and L. Giorgianni. (n.d.). "MARKET OUTLOOK – MACRO PERSPECTIVE."

Kirkpatrick, C., and J. Dahlquist. (2006). *Technical Analysis: The Complete Resource for Financial Market Technicians*. First edition. Upper Saddle River, NJ: FT Press.

Kraken Intelligence. (n.d.). "Proof-of-Work vs Proof-of-Stake—Securing the Chain." https://kraken.docsend.com/view/2gwc64da9h5ccmhm.

Kuepper, J. (2019). "Using Genetic Algorithms to Forecast Financial Markets." Investopedia.

Lin, L., L. Cao, J. Wang, and C. Zhang. (2004). "The Applications of Genetic Algorithms in Stock Market Data Mining Optimisation." Management Information Systems [Conference Proceeding], December 1, 2004. http://hdl.handle.net/10453/7024.

Makarov, D., and A. Schoar. (2022). "Cryptocurrencies and Decentralized Finance (DeFi)."

Marshall, B. (2018). "What Is the Math Behind Elliptic Curve Cryptography?" https://hackernoon.com/what-is-the-math-behind-elliptic-curve-cryptography-f61b25253da3.

Marshall, B. (2019). "How Does ECDSA Work in Bitcoin?" https://medium.com/@blairlmarshall/how-does-ecdsa-work-in-bitcoin-7819d201a3ec.

Murphy, J. (1999). *Technical Analysis of the Financial Markets*. New York: New York Institute of Finance.

Nakamoto, S. (2008). "Bitcoin: A Peer-to-Peer Electronic Cash System." https://bitcoin.org/bitcoin.pdf.

Nison, S. (1991). *Japanese Candlestick Charting Techniques*. Saddle River, NJ: Prentice Hall.

O'Toole, D. (2019). "How to Build an Automated Trading System." https://www.investopedia.com/articles/active-trading/101014/how-build-automated-trading-system.asp.

Pring, M. (2002). *Technical Analysis Explained*. 5th edition. New York: McGraw Hill Education.

ProfileTraders. (n.d.). "Jesse Livermore Quotes: 10 Powerful Lessons and Trading Rules." https://www.profiletraders.in/post/jesse-livermore-quotes-10-powerful-lessons-and-trading-rules.

Rhea, R. (1932). *The Dow Theory*. New York: Barron's.

Shiffman, D. (2012). *The Nature of Code: Simulating Natural Systems with Process-ing.* 1st edition. https://natureofcode.com/.

Smith, A. (2018). "How to Convert Trading Strategies into Forex Robots." https://www.dailyforex.com/forex-articles/2018/09/how-to-convert-trading-strategies-into-forex-robots/101029.

Smith, N. (2020). "Vitalik Buterin: Stock-to-Flow Bitcoin Price Model 'Really Not Looking Good Now.'" https://decrypt.co/103424/vitalik-buterin-stock-to-flow-bitcoin-price-model-really-not-looking-good-now.

Straßburg, Janko, Christian Gonzàlez-Martel, and Vassil Alexandrov. "Parallel Genetic Algorithms for Stock Market Trading Rules." *Procedia Computer Science* 9 (2012):1306–1313.

Tongia, R. (n.d.). "The Dark Side of Metcalfe's Law: Multiple and Growing Costs of Network Exclusion."

Van de Poppe, P. (2020). "PLAN B—Stock to Flow."

Van Vliet, B. (2012). *Building Automated Trading Systems: With an Introduction to Visual C++.NET.* First edition. Amsterdam: Elsevier.

Wikipedia. (2022). "Metcalfe's Law." https://en.wikipedia.org/wiki/Metcalfe%27s_law.

Wilder, J.W. (1978). *New Concepts in Technical Trading Systems.* Trend Research.

Author Bio

Eoghan Leahy, BA, MBS, MSc, CAIA, CMT, MSTA
I am the founder and managing director of Quant Market Intelligence Limited, an AI-powered trading and research company. I also volunteer as the chair of the CMT Association UAE chapter.

As the former quantitative technical analysis and cryptocurrency specialist for Bloomberg, I was fortunate to collaborate on strategy development projects with many professional clients across Europe, the Middle East, and Africa (EMEA).

While at Bloomberg, I pioneered the promotion of automated cryptocurrency trading techniques, publishing several articles, an award-winning research report, and delivering hundreds of popular presentations across the EMEA region.

In 2018 I left Bloomberg to undertake a second masters' degree in high performance computing at Trinity College Dublin. I then founded a quant trading company that leverages distributed genetic algorithms to optimize trading systems. These techniques have been used to develop the Bitcoin AlphaBot™ automated trading system.

I hope this book will help readers to develop robust risk-managed trading strategies and automated systems. While the primary focus is on

Bitcoin prices, the techniques are applicable across financial markets and asset classes.

Over many years helping hedge funds, sovereign wealth funds, and treasury departments backtest and automate trading signals, I developed a broad knowledge of the effective approaches employed by Bloomberg's elite clients. It is these lessons that this book will share.

Index

Page numbers followed by *f* refer to figures.

U

Uptrends, 62, 66
US dollar, 32, 43*f*, 46, 84*f*, 88*f*, 148*f*, 152*f*
US Federal Reserve, 3, 4, 4*f*, 150, 151*f*
US national debt, 3, 4, 5*f*

V

Variation, 123
Vectors, 124
Ver, Roger, 15
Visa, 8
Visual recognition, 66
Volatility, 131, 138

Volume:
  in Dow theory, 62
  in quantitative analysis, 104

W

Wallets, 19
Wall Street Journal, 57, 68
Web 3.0, 14
Weighted moving averages, 72
Wilde, Oscar, 35
Wilder, J. Welles, Jr., 73, 74

Y

Yield, 29